Cheraw District, South Carolina, Court of Equity

Volume 3: Minutes, 1833-1837

Lee G. Barrow

Available from Amazon.com and other retailers
www.createspace.com/4990490

Also available direct from the author:
Lee G. Barrow
4071 Ada Creek Drive
Gainesville, GA 30506

Bargraphica, Gainesville, GA
www.bargraphica.com/books
v1.0 September 2014

International Standard Book Number
ISBN-13: 978-1502312709
ISBN-10: 1502312700
Reference/Genealogy

Cheraw District, South Carolina, Court of Equity

Volume 3:
Minutes, 1833-1837

Lee G. Barrow

Preface

This book is a complete transcription of the Court of Equity minutes for Cheraw District, South Carolina, for the years 1833 to 1837, transcribed from a microfilm copy of the original book purchased from the South Carolina State Archives. At the time, the district included present-day Chesterfield, Darlington, Marlboro and portions of Florence and Lee Counties.

The author has attempted to copy these minutes in such a way to be as readable as possible while remaining faithful to what is found in the original. Most misspellings and obvious errors have been entered as they appear in the original with the apparent mistake <u>underlined</u>; archaic spellings (such as "shew") have been entered without indication. Text which has been crossed out in the original has been entered herein and ~~struck through~~. Some punctuation marks, such as commas between names, have been added to improve clarity. All names have been set in **bold** in order to assist the reader in locating them. The full-name index combines like-sounding names and includes cross references to accommodate different spelling variations.

In the original book, the writing is sometimes difficult to read and different letters sometimes look much the same. There are also many cases where the clerk made an obvious mistake or spelled the same person's name differently in different places. It is also possible that I made a few transcription errors. The reader is encouraged to refer to the original document whenever possible. If you find something you believe to be a mistake, I welcome your comments or corrections.

Symbols

The following symbols are used in the text:

[?]   A question mark indicates that the original was very diffi-
        cult to read and the word entered represents the author's
        best guess.

\ /   Slashes enclose text which was inserted in the original as
        an afterthought or a correction.

[ ]   Brackets enclose text added by the transcriber, either as an
        assumption of missing or unreadable text or as a comment.

)
)   Right parentheses over one another represent wavy vertical
)   lines.

Cheraw District, South Carolina, Court of Equity
Volume 3: Minutes, 1833-1837

This is the third portion of the first book of minutes for the Cheraw Court of Equity.
The first two portions were transcribed in Volumes 1 and 2 of this series.

February Term 1833

At a Court of Equity holden at Darlington Court House for the District of Cheraw the 18th February 1833 present the Honorable **Job Johnson** Eqr. one of the Cancellors of said State.

Exparte Th*ee* Master &   ) In Cheraw 18th Feby. 1833
Commissioner in Equity) It is ordered by the Court that the Commissioner of this Court do furtherwith make a Report to the Court of the different Estate in his hands under and by virtue of any Decree or order of the Court with a full & particular account of the monies & paid Relating to the Said Estate and that he ~~Double~~ do forth*e*with Report what Guardians or Trustees have not annually made Returns of all monies received & expended and which of them have so made their Returns The said Commissioner accompanying his Return with such observations on the accounts of the said guardians & Trustees as may be necessary & conducive to Justice that the said Commr. do also Report what guardians Trustees Executors & administrators have been ordered by any provision Decree or order of the Court to account annually setting forth which of them have complied, which of them have failed to comply therewith That he also Report upon all Estate in his own hand as receiver with a full & particular account of his rec*ei*ts & expenditures and other proceedings in relation thereto That his further report all sales made by him or by his predecessor in office in obedience to any order or Decree of the Court and which ~~of them~~ \have/ ~~two~~ not been heretofore reported to and undergone the final Decision of the Court stating in such reports what property was sold, when, to whom, the time, the creditors, and what terms or securities have been taken to secure the purchase money that he report also Estate if any are in ~~danager~~ \danger/ of suffering loss or injury by reason of the [*crossout*] \insolvency/ or doubtful credits of the guardian, Trustees or Receiver in whose hand the sum may be or by reason of the insolvency or Doubtful credit of their Securities or any of them or from any other case whatever.   **Job Johnston**

No. 1. On motion of Mr. **Blanding** Solicitor for **Edmund W. Gregg** ordered that that the Commissioner enquire and report whether the said **E. W. Gregg** has attained the age of Twenty one years and if so whether it [*crossout*] proper for the Guardian to pay over to him the income of his wifes Estate as stated in the return of his guardian **Nathaniel L. Edgeworth.**

Job Johnston

Page 382   _February 1833_

February Term 1833

Exparte   ) Petition for Guardianship
Elisha Baker) The petition being read in this case It is ordered on motion of Mr. **Blanding** for the petitioner that it be refered to the Commissioner to report whether it is proper that the prayer thereof shall be granted and what is the annual value on income of the minor Estate and in what sum security ought to be required.   **Job Johnston**

Exparte   ) No. 3
James Moore) Petition for Guardianship
by next friend) On motion of Mr. **Moses** Solicitor for petitioner ordered that it be refered to the Commissioner to enquire into the propriety of the appointment prayed for and the gross value of the Estate to which the infant may be entitled and that the said Commissioner do report thereon.

Job Johnston

Exparte   ) No. 4 Petition for Guardianship
Simeon Jas. Chapman) On motion of **Graham** Sol. ordered that it be refered to the commissioner to asertain & report the age & gross value of the Estate of the Petitioners and whether the said **D. T. G. Graham** is a suitable person to be appointed Guardian.   **Job Johnston**

Expart **Mary**) No. 5 Petition for guardianship
C. Chapman) On motion of **Graham** ordered that it be refered to the Commissioner to asertain & report whether the facts stated in the Petition is true that he asertain & report the age (and gross of value of the Estate) of the petitioners and whether the said the **Alex. Graham** is a suitable person to be appointed Guardian.   **Job Johnston**

Sheppard Williams) No. 6
ordinary   )
    vs.   ) Bill for accounts & Partition
Sarah Hill & others) On motion that **Geo. W. Dargan** Commissioner of this Court be appointed guardian ad Litum for the Infant Defendants in this Case.   **Job Johnston**

February Term 1833

Exparte   ) No. 7
James M. Norwood) It appearing from the report of the Commissioner
that **James M. Norwood** has attained the age of twenty one years on motion
ordered that **A. D. Sims** the Guardian of said **James M. Norwood** do settle
his accounts with his Ward and upon his so settling to satisfaction of the
Commissioner of this Court <u>Court</u> that he be Dis<u>charg</u>ed from making
further returns.   **Job Johnston**

Exparte **Accey**) No. 8
Grice an Idiot) The Commissioner to whom was Directed a writ in the
matters of a writ de Lunatico inquirendo having Certified to the Court their
proceedings under the same and the finding of the Jury that the said **Accey**
Grice is an Idiot and has been so from her Infancy and is totally unable to
conduct her self or manage her<u>s</u>elf with ~~ordering~~ ordinary Judgment and
Discretion and that she has an Estate of about the value of six hundred and
seventy Dollars It is on motion of Mr. **Jas. R. Ervin** Solicitor for the Petitioner ordered that it be refered to the Commissioner to enquire and report
who should be appointed the Committee of the said **Accey Grice** and the
amount of the security necessary to be given.   **Job Johnston**

T. Dargan & wife & alii   ) No. 9
     vs.   )
Sarah T. Zimmerman & al) The Commissioner having made a report of
sales of personal property ordered to be sold at the last Court It is ordered on
motion of Mr. **Ervin** Solicitor for Complainants that the report be confirmed.
                                             Job Johnston

Mary Woods & others   ) No. 10
     vs.   )
Geo. W. Dargan Exors. & others) On motion ordered that it be refered to
A. M. McIver Esq. to enquire into and report upon the expediency of selling
the Negroes and Lands allotted in this case to the children of **A. B. Woods** by
his first wife.   **Job Johnston**

February Term 1833

John Evans   ) No. 11
     vs.   ) Bill for Sale of Lands
Exor. **Saml. Evans** & others) It is on motion of **McIver** Solicitor for Complainants ordered that the Bill be Dismissed.   **Job Johnston**

Taylor & McQueen) No. 12
vs.   )
Thos. J. Williams) On motion of **Coit** ordered that the Report of the Commissioner of Sales be Confirmed.   **Job Johnston**

William McQueen   ) No. 13
vs.   )
Margaret McQueen et al) On motion of **Coit** & **Phillips** ordered that the order for sale heretofore made in the above case be extended.
        Job Johnston

David Davis & wife   ) No. 14
vs.   )
Covington Massey & others) On motion of **Graham** Solicitor for Def<u>l</u>ts. ordered that the Bill ~~be~~ in this case be Discharged.
        Job Johnston

R. A. Pettigrew & wife) No. 15
vs.   ) Bill for Partition & a/c
John Chambliss & others) On motion of **Sims** ordered that the Report of the Commissioner in this case be confirmed.   **Job Johnston**

R. A. Pettigrew & wife) No. 16
vs.   ) Bill for Account & Partition
John Chambliss & others) On motion of **Sims** Complts. Solicitor It is ordered and Decreed that the Report of the Commissioner in this case appointed to Divide the Estate in the Bill mentioned be Confirmed and that the share allotted to **R. A. Pettigrew** & wife be settled before the wife of the said **Pettigrew** to her sole & sep<u>e</u>rate use During her life and to the Children of the Marriage afterwards share & share alike and the Commissioner see that the Deed of Sett<u>lm</u>ent

Page 385 _____ *February 1833*
                        February Term 1833

in accordance with this order be duly executed and ~~and~~ together with the Decree Recorded according to Law.   **Job Johnston**

Exparte   ) No. 17
James Moore)
by next friend) On considering the report made on above petition and the said **James & Henry** being examined in open Court ordered that the same be confirmed and that **Henry Moore** be appointed Guardian of the Estate of said **James Moore** on his giving Bond with Security in Double the amount of the value of his Estate as therein reported.   **Job Johnston**

Exparte   ) No. 8
Commr. in Equity) Report on **John Dewitt** guardian of **Jno. D. McCollough**
Ordered that the Report be received & Confirmed but in as much as the
guardian Did not Report in Due time nor until he was this day reported as a
Defaulter It is ordered that he be deprived of his ~~com~~ Comm. for the time
Covered by his Return.   **Job Johnston**

Rosanna Lance) No. 19
    vs.   )
Thos. C. Lance) On motion of **Coit** & **Phillips** ordered that the order ~~h~~
heretofore made in this case for the creditors of **Jno. G. Lance** decd. to prove
their demands before the Commr. of this Court be extended & ~~may~~ any
creditors be permitted to prove their Demands during the first day of the
present term of this Court.   **Job Johnston**

James Gillispie & wife   ) No. 20
    vs.   ) Partition
Jno. J. Marshall & wife et al) The Commr. having reported sales of Land in
Bill mentioned it is ordered on motion of **McIver** that the Report be con-
firmed.   **Job Johnston**

Exrs. **Thomas**   ) No. 21
    vs.   )
Margaret Alson)
William Alson) The Commissioner having Reported

Page 386   *February 1833*
                        February Term 1833

on sales made by him in this case in the above case It is on motion of **Coit** &
Phillips ordered that the Report be confirmed.   **Job Johnston**

Robt. B. Campbell &   ) No. 22
Wm. Pennywell & others)
    vs.   )
R. B. Wiggins and   )
Jonathan Pennywell   ) The Commissioner having submitted his Report
of sales of the Real Estate of **Mason Lee** Decd. It is ordered that the same be
Confirmed – except as to the purchase of **J. W. Lester** on which the Decision
of the Court is suspended.   **Job Johnston**

Isaiah DuBose   ) No. 23
    vs.   )
Martha Muse et al) On motion of **Coit** & **Phillips** Solicitor for Complainants It is ordered that the Report ~~be~~ of the Commr. in this case made by him
in the above case be confirmed.   **Job Johnston**

Moses Sanders   ) No. 24
vs.   )
Wm. Law & others   ) The Commr. having made a Report of Sales ~~of~~ ordered
on motion of **Wilkins** that the same ~~same~~ be confirmed as relates to **Samuel
B. Wilkins** who has complyed with the terms of Sale.

Job Johnston

Exparte   ) No. 25
Robert Reynolds) The Commissioner having Reported that **Robert Reynolds** heretofore appointed guardian of the property of his Infant Children
has not yet qualified as Guardian It is on motion of **Wilkins** ordered that the
said **Robert Reynolds** have leave to give Bond and Security During this week.

Job Johnston

John Taylor   ) No. 26
vs.   )
Wm. Johnson et al)

Page 387   *February 1833*

February Term 1833

On motion of **Coit** & **Phillips** ordered that the Report of the Commissioner
~~in~~ sales made by him in this case be confirmed.   **Job Johnston**

Thos. B. Poindexter & wife) No. 27
vs.   )
H. Zimmerman   ) On motion of **Simes** ordered that the Commissioners Report ~~in~~ sales made by him in this case be confirmed.

Job Johnston

Nancy Horn   ) No. 28
vs.   )
Henry Horn & others) It is on motion of **Coit** & **Phillips** Solicitor for
Complets. that the report of the Commissioner ~~in~~ sales made in Bill in the
above case be confirmed.   **Job Johnston**

Gavin Witherspoon   ) No. 29
admr. of **H. Thompson**)
vs.   ) Bill to enjoin creditors and marshall assets
The Creditors of **H.**   )
Thompson Decd.   ) On motion of **Wilkins** & with Consent of **Ervin**
for Complainant It is ordered that the case be reinstated on the Docket and
that the Commissioner enquire into and Report the Dividends to which the
creditors are entitled.   **Job Johnston**

Exparte) \No. 30/ Petition for leave to sell Land
Henry Moore) On hearing the Petition on motion of Mr. **Moses** Solicitor for Petitioner ordered that it be Refered to the Commissioner to report on the facts of said petition that he also report the price at which the Land can be sold – the adequacy of the same ~~amount~~ and the advantage of selling the same resulting to the minor.   **Job Johnston**

Daniel Myers & others	) No. 31
vs.	)
Asa Hyram Stuart & wife	)
& others Exors. **Danl. Myers**	)
& others	) On motion of **Sims**

Page 388   _February 1833_

February Term 1833

Complts. Sol. it is ordered that he have leave to amend the Bill in this case During the sitting of this Court also ordered that **Asa Hyram Stuart** & wife & **James Myers** who appear by the affidavit of **Levi Gray** to be absent from & without the limits of this state do appear & answer plead or Demur to said amended Bill on or before the first day of August next & that in Default thereof the said Bill be taken pro confesso against them further ordered that this Notice be published twice a month for the space of Three months in the Cheraw Republican prior to the first of August next.

Job Johnston

Wm. McQueen	) No. 32
vs.	)
Mary McQueen	)
& others	) On motion of Mr. **Graham** ordered that the report of the

Commr. ~~to~~ on sales made by him in this case be confirmed.

Job Johnston

Rebecca Cosnahan	) No. 33
& others	)
vs.	)
David Mandiville	) By order of the Court Dated 15th day of February 1832

among other things It is ordered that the Commissioner of this Court do collect \the/amount of **John Rogers** Bond given for the purchase of a tract of Land the subject of Partition in Bill mentioned and when he received the same his is ordered to pay the same to the parties inter~~s~~ted or their l~~a~~gal ~~represented~~ representatives It is now on motion of Mr. **Ervin** Solicitor for Complainant ordered that the Commissioner of this Court do vest so much of the funds as is due to the Complainant and who are minors without guardians at interest and that he take Bond & Security And on motion of Mr. **Graham** it is ordered that the Commissioner of the Defendant do pay over to the Administrator of the Defendant **David Mandevill** the amount ~~of~~ in his hand arising from the sale ~~to which~~ of Land in the above stated case to which the said Defendant is entitled.   **Job Johnston**

Page 389 _____ _February 1833_
                              February Term 1833

The Court then Adjourned to ten oclock Tomorrow Morning.

Tuesday Morning Ten oclock Present the Honorable **Job Johnson** Esquire.

The Court met Pursuant to Adjournment.

Expart The   ) \No. 1/ Report on Estate
Commr. in Equity) Ordered that the Report remain on file to await the motion of persons Interested.   **Job Johnston**

Expartite The   ) No. 2 Report on De_fa_lting Guardian
Commr. in Equity) Ordered that the Guardians reported for not giving Bond & security ~~show case~~ \shew cause/ at the next term why their ~~appointed~~ appointment should not be revoked except **Robert Reynolds** & **John Dewitt** on whose cases an order was made yesterday ordered that the guardian who are reported for failure to ~~to~~ make annual returns be Deprived ~~of the Defendant~~ \of their commissions in the time covered by their default and/ that they shew cause ~~why~~ at the next term why they should not be attached or otherwise Dealt with at the Discretion of the Court for their Defaults and that the rules now pending against them be extended to the next Term.
                              Job Johnston

Ordered that \No. 3/ the Register make out for the use of the Court at each term a sep_e_rate Docket for Petition whereon no cause shall be set over until Due proof to be to be endorse on the _petion_ of its having been s_e_ved on the opposite party until the record shall have been made up by an order pro confesso or other Definitive pleading.   **Job Johnston**

Ordered that the Register keep in Court at Each term an extra Docket for the use of the bar of all cases pending at said term whether on Bill or Petition.
                              Job Johnston

Rosanna Lance   ) No. 4
   vs.   )
Thos. T. Lance et al)

Page 390   *February 1833*
                              February Term 1833

On motion of **Coit** & **Phillips** ordered that it be refe<u>rd</u> to the Commr. to examine & Report whether it is necessary to sell the Real Estate in Bill mentioned for the payment of the debts of the intestate It is also ordered that **Geo. W. Dargan** the Comr. of this Court be appointed Guardian ad Litem to **Thomas C. Lance** an infant Defendant & that he answer the Bill.
                                                              Job Johnston

John C. Coit admr.)
2) vs.   )
James Coit Et al   ) On motion ordered that the accounts of **J. C. Coit** admr. be refered to the Commr. & that he Report thereon.
                                                              Job Johnston

A. Nesbitt admr.   )
3) vs.   )
Joseph Pearson et al) On motion it is ordered that it ~~beref~~ be refered to the Comr. to examine & Report upon the Sales which have been made in this case & also to report the amount funds in his hands applicable & also the manner in which the funds should be ap<u>pie</u>d to some Debts.
                                                              Job Johnston

M. B. Alson) No. 4
     vs.   ) Bill to marshall Assets
W. B. Alson)
et allos   ) On motion **Coit** & **Phillips** ordered that the Report made in this case Yesterday by the Commissioner be confirmed.
                                                              Job Johnston

A. B. Alson admr.   )
Joseph Pearson   )
     vs.   ) Bill to Marshall Assets
W. T. Alson Heirs &   )
Creditors of **Joseph Alson**) 5) On motion of **Graham** Solicitor & by Consent of Mr. **Coit** it is ordered that the Commr. of this court ~~be~~ do pay over to **Margarett**

Page 391   *February 1833*
                              February Term 1833

B. Alson the sum reported to be Due her for her dower in the Real Estate of **Joseph Alson** decd. which was sold by order of this Court on her execu<u>tt</u>ing titles to **Charles Vanderford** and **Cornelaus Lynch** for the Lots of Land purchased by them.   **Job Johnston**

Exparte   ) Petition for Guardianship
Thomas E. Lance) 6) On motion of **Coit** ordered that ~~the~~ it be refered to the Commissioner to investigate and report upon the gross amount of the Estate to which the petitioner is entitled to and also whether **Rosanna Troy** be a proper person to be appointed as guardian of said petition.
                   Job Johnston

Exparte   )
Thomas C. Lance) On motion of **Coit** It is ordered that letters of Guardianship be given to **Rosanna Troy** as guardian of the Estate of **Thomas C. Lance** upon her lodging with the Commissioner Bond & Security in treble the amount of the petitioners Estate as Reported.
                   Job Johnston

Exors. of **Wm. F. Ellerbe**)
      vs.   ) Bill
C. Prince & wife & others) 7) On motion ordered that the Commissioner of this Court be appointed guardian ad Litum of the Infant Defendants **Alex R. Ellerbe** and **Thos. R. Ellerbe**.   **Job Johnston**

Exparte   ) Petition for guardian
William Peacock) 8 The Petition<u>er</u> in this case having been <u>red</u> It is ordered that it be refered to the Commissioner to Report whether the petitioner is a fit person to be the guardian of the minors what is the value of their Estate and in what sums security ought to be ~~regauard~~ required.
                   Job Johnston

Exparte, **Axcey**)
Grice an Idiot) The Commissioner having reported and recommended that **Wade Grice** be appointed

February Term 1833

9) the Committee of the said **Axcey Grice** and that he give Bond & Security in the penal sum of Two Thousand Dollars It is on motion of Mr. **Ervin** Sol. for the petitioner ordered that **Wade Grice** ~~be appointed~~ be appointed the Committee of the ~~same~~ said **Axcey** upon his giving Bond with security Commissioner of this Court in the penal sum of Two thousand Dollars conditioned for the faithful fulfilment of the trust confided to him as committee of said Idiot.   **Job Johnston**

Exparte   ) Petition for time to sell Land
Henry Moore) 10) The Commissioner having made his Report upon this Petition on motion of Mr. **Moses** Solicitor for petitioner ordered that the

same be confirmed and that the said **Henry Moore** Guardian of **Jas. Moore** be allowed to sell & convey the tract of land owned by said **James** at the price stated in said report and that he be authorized as guardian to make a title of the same to the purchaser.   **Job Johnston**

Exparte   ) Petition for Guardianship
Joseph Cosnahan) 11) On motion of **McIver** it is ordered that it be refered to the Commissioner of this Court to enquire whether ~~Edmond~~ **Edward Cosnahan** be a Suitable person to be appointed Guardian of the person & property of **Joseph Cosnahan** the age of the said **Joseph** and the gross value of the Estate.   **Job Johnston**

Exparte   ) Petition for guardian
Wesley Freling) 12) The petition for this case having been filed It is on motion of Mr. **Ervin** Solicitor for petition ordered that it be Refered to the Commissioner to enquire & report upon the propriety of appointing **Joel C. DuBose** the guardian of the Estate of the Petitioner and of the Gross value thereof and upon the facts stated in the Petition.
                Job Johnston

Exparte **Wm. H.**   )
Cannon Guardian)
of **John J. Cannon**) On motion of **Coggeshall** Solicitor for **Wm. H. Cannon** ordered that it be refered to the Commissioner

February Term 1833

13) of this Court to enquire & report whether it would be for the Infant benefit to diliver up to the guardian a Bond belonging to the Estate of the Infant given by **George W. Moy** & **William L. Moye** for the purchase of a tract of land at the Commissioner thereof the Bond of the Guardian & his security should not be increased and to what amount.
                Job Johnston

C. Pegues & wife   )
     vs.   )
E. J. Cosnahan & others) 14 On motion of **McIver** it is ordered that it be refered to the Commissioner of this Court to report upon the accounts of **Edward J. Cosnahan** administrator & als to enquire whether the sale heretofore made by said administrator of Nine years to **Arthur Pearce** is for the benefit of the parties ~~Intestated~~ interested.   **Job Johnston**

Christopher Pegues & wife)
vs.   ) Bill for Partition & Account
Edwd. J. Cosnahan   )
Sarah Cosnahan   )
Joseph Cosnahan   ) 15 On motion of **McIver** it is ordered that ~~it be~~ **George W. Dargan** Commissioner of this Court be ~~a~~ appointed guardian ad Litem for **Sarah Cosnahan** and **Edward Cosnahan** Infant Defendants in the above stated case and that he do answer to Complainants Bill.
                                        Job Johnston

A. Nesbitt Heirs   )
vs.   )
A. Jesse Pearson et al) On motion of **Coit** & **Phillips** It is ordered that the report of the Commissioner in the above case be confirmed.
                                        Job Johnston

Rosanna Lance   )
vs.   )
Thos. C. Lance et al) 17 On motion of **Coit** & **Phillips** it is ordered that the report of the Commissioner in the above case be confirmed.
                                        Job Johnston

<u>*Page 394*</u>   <u>*February 1833*</u>
                            February Term 1833

Exparte   )
Eliza Ann Hill, Martha C. Hill   )
Emily E. Hill, Harriet C. Hill   ) Petition
John Quincy Hill, Sarah J. Hill &) for
Margaret Frances Hill by their   ) Guardianship
next friend **James King**   ) 18 On motion of **Sims** ordered that it be Refered to the Commissioner to Report whether the said **James King** is a suitable person to be appointed guardian according to the prayer of the petitioners and also to what Estate the petitioners are entitled and for what sum the said Guardian should give Security.   **Job Johnston**

Exparte **Eliza**   ) Petition for Guardianship
Ann Hill & others) 19 On motion of **Sims** it is ordered that **James King** be appointed guardian of the person and Estate of the petitioners upon his giving Bond & security to the Commissioner of this Court in treble the amount of the Estate of the petitioners and said Bond conditioned according to Law.   **Job Johnston**

Exors. **Thomas**   )
vs.   )
Peter E. Graves) 20 On motion of **Coit** & **Phillips** It is ordered that the report ~~of~~ in the above case be confirmed.   **Job Johnston**

S. William ordinary)
   vs.   )
Sarah Hill & others) 21   On motion of **Simes** Complts. Solicitor It is ordered that so much of the Bill as prays for the sale of Land & personal Estate be Refered to the Commissioner of this Court be Reported upon the propriety of granting such prayer.   **Job Johnston**

Levi & J. Hickson)
   vs.   ) Bill of Complaint
Robert Fraser & alii)

Page 395   _February 1833_
February Term 1833

On motion of Mr. **Ervin** Solicitor of Complainants ordered that the Commission issued & returned in this case do pass publication upon the trial of this case. [_in margin:_] 22   **Job Johnston**

Burrell Brewer   ) [_in margin:_] 23
   vs.   ) Bill to confirm title to reale Estate
Wm. N. Peacok & others) On hearing the Bill in this case & the answer of the minor Defendant by their guardian ad Litem it is ordered that it be refered to the Commissioner to \report/ whether it will be for the interest of the infant Defendant to confirm the sale made to the Complainants on securing to the minor Defendant their shear of the purchase money and the manner in which the same should be se secured to them.
                           Job Johnston

Elizabeth McGraw) [_in margin:_] 24
by Guardian   )
John Nicholson &)
A. Johnson   ) On motion of **Graham** Solicitor It is ordered that the order pro confesso be set a side and the Defendant have leave to plead answer or demur in thirty Days provided deft. be not allowed to plead \a/ Delatory plea.   **Job Johnston**

Elizabeth McGraw) [_in margin:_] 25
by Guardian   )
John Nicholson   )
& **A. Johnson**   ) On motion of Mr. **Moses** Complainant Solr. ordered that he have leave to file the exhibits A. B. C. D. & E. with the original Bill.
                           Job Johnston

Exparte   )
S. J. Chapman) On motion of **Graham** ordered that the Report of the Commissioner be confirmed and that **G. Graham** be appointed guardian of the person & property of Petitioner on his giving Bond and security in the sum of Five thosand Dollars.   **Job Johnston**

February Term 1833

Expart~~in~~   ) [*in margin:*] 26
M. C. Chapman) on motion of **Graham** ordered that the Report of the
Commissioner be confirmed and that said **Alexander Graham** be appointed
guardian of the person & property of the Petitioner on his giving Bond and
Security in the sum of five th~~os~~and Dollars.   **Job Johnston**

Levi Hickson &   )
John Hickson   )
      vs.   )
C. Clement & **Robt. Fraser**) This case heard.

The Court then Adjourned to 10 oclock To morrow morning.

Wednesday morning 20 Feby. 1833. Court ~~then~~ met pursuant to adjournment.

Exparte   ) [*in margin:*] 1
Elisha Baker) The Commi~~s~~ioner having submi~~t~~ed his report in this Petition It is ordered that **Elisha Baker** be appointed guardian of his wife **Sarah**
on ~~complainant~~ complying with the terms expressed in the report & that in
such appointment **N. L. Edgeworth** is Dismissed from further acting in his
Guardianship.   **Job Johnston**

Exparte   ) [*in margin:*] 2
Joseph Cosnahan) The Commissioner having reported that **Edward J.
Cosnahan** is a proper person to be appointed guardian of **Joseph Cosnahan**
it is ~~of~~ on motion of **McIver** ordered that the said **Edward J. Cosnahan** be
appointed guardian of the \said/ **Joseph ~~Joseph~~ Cosnahan** upon his giving
Bond & Security in the sum of twenty two thousand & five hundred dollars.
                                                  Job Johnston

February Term 1833

Christopher Pegues & wife)
      vs.   ) Bill for a/c & Partition
Edwd. J. Cosnahan   )
Sarah Cosnahan   )
Jos. Cosnahan   ) The Commissioner having reported in the
above Case it is ordered on motion of **McIver** Complainants Solicitor ord-
ered that the report be confirmed.   **Job Johnston**

Mary Woods & an other)
   vs.   )
Geo. W. Dargan Exr.   )
A. B. Woods & others   ) The report of **A M. McIver** ~~th~~ the referee having been[?] ordered that the same be confirmed and that the recommendation of said report be made the order of this Court.   **Job Johnston**

Clement D. Wallace   )
William D. Wallace   )
Thomas S. Wallace   )
   vs.   ) Bill for Partition or Sale
E. A. Ellerbe &   )
M. A. Wallace & others) on motion of Mr. **Blanding** Complainants Solicitor It is ordered that it be refered to the Commissioner to enquire and report whether it will be most for the benefit of the parties interested in the Real Estate of **Thomas F. Ellerbe** Deceased & **Rebecca Ann Ellerbe** Deceased to have the same sold ~~o~~ under the Decree of the Court or to have the Lands Divided and the reason[?] of his Report in this publication[?].

                                       Job Johnston

L. Prince &   )
Is. DuBose   )
   vs.   ) Bill to Foreclose Mortgage
C. D. Wallace) On motion of **Wilkins** It is ordered that Complainants have leave to Discontinue their Bill upon Defts. paying the Costs of the Same.

                                       Job Johnston

Page 398   *February 1833*
                    February Term 1833

James Hunter   ) 6
   vs.   )
Jn. Brown   )
William Hunter   )
Averulla[?] **Hunter**   ) Bill
Isabella Hunter   )
Martha Hunter   )
Washington Hunter)
Caroline Blackwell   ) On motion of Mr. **Blanding** Complainant Solicitor ordered that the Commissioner of this Court be appointed guardian ad Litem of the above named Defts. who are Infants under the age of twenty one years.

                                       Job Johnston

J. C. Coit adm.   ) 7
   vs.   )
Joh*athan Coit et al) It is ordered on motion of **Coit & Phillips** Complainants Sol. that the report of the Commissioner in the above case be confirmed.
[*in margin:*] *a true copy   **Job Johnston**

The Exors. of **W. F. Ellerbe** decd.) 8
   vs.   ) Bill of Complainants
Clement Prince & wife   )
William T. Ellerbe   )
Alex R. Ellerbe   )
Thomas R. Ellerbe   ) on motion of Mr. **Blanding** Complainants Solicitor It is ordered that the Commissioner enquire & report whether
it is necessary & proper that the tracts of Land & [*crossout*] mills purchased
by the Complainants testator & **George T. Hearsey** should be sold & the
proceed applied ~~th~~ to the payment of the testators Debts & whether it is
proper that any of \the/ slaves of the Estate should be sold for the payment of
the Debts of the Estate.   **Job Johnston**

Exparte   ) 9
Edmund W. Gregg) The Commissioner having submitted his report it is
ordered that the same be Confirmed.   **Job Johnston**

Page 399   *February 1833*
                  February Term 1833

Christopher Pegues & wife) 11
   vs.   )
Edward J. Cosnahan   )
Sarah Cosnahan   )
Joseph Cosnahan   ) on motion of **McIver** Complaints Sol. it is
ordered that a writ of partition do issue in this case to be directed to **David
Crossland, Alex McIntosh, James A. Forniss, W. Crossland, Jno. McCul-
lom** directing them to proceed & Di~~vid~~ the Estate in Bill mentioned according to the legal interest of the parties.   **Job Johnston**

Samuel Goodwin & wife)
   vs.   & others   ) 12
L. B. Bright & others   ) The Commissioners made in this writ of Partition issued in this case to Divide and make partition of the personal estate of
Charles Bright in Bill mentioned having made & returned to this court their
partition It is on motion of **Ervine & Robbins** Solicitors for Complainants
ordered that their return be confirmed It is further ordered that a writ of
Partition do issue from this Court Directed to **John McCollum, Jno.
Donaldson, Charles J. Lide, James Irby** and **Henry Easterling** authorizing &

requiring them to Divid & make partition of the real estate in Bill mentioned and that their partition and Division under their hands and ~~do m~~ seals thy return to the next Court of Equity for Cheraw District It is further ordered that so much of the personal Estait as is partitioned to the Defendant **L. B. Bright** be reclaimed until the final settlement of his accounts as administrator of **Charles Bright** & that the said be charged with whait ever may appear to be due by him.   **Job Johnston**

Barrell Brewer) 13
        vs.   ) Bill to Confirm the titles to real Estate
W. N. Peacock)
& others   ) The Commissioner having Submmitted his report in this case on motion of Mr. **Blanding** Complainants Solicitor it is ordered that the same be confirmed and he make a Decree of this Court and that the costs be paid out of the shares of the Infant Dendants.

                        February Term 1833

Exparte **Wm.**) 14 Petition for guardianship
N. Peacock   ) The Commissioner having ~~sb~~ submitted his report on this petition It is ordered that the same be confirmed and that the said **Wm. N. Peacock, Calvin Peacock, Washington Peacock** & **Caroline Peacock** on his complying with the terms mentioned in the said report.
                                        Job Johnston

Elizabeth McLean) No. 15
by Guardian   )
        vs.   ) Bill
John Nicholson   )
& **A. Johnson**   ) On motion of Mr. **Moses** for Complts. ~~plain~~ and Mr. **Graham** for Defendants ordered that this case be ~~con~~ refered to the Commissioner to report upon the State of the accounts. **Job Johnston**

Elizabeth McLean by)
guardian **N. McLeod**)
        vs.   ) Bill
John Nicholson &   )
A. Johnson   ) The Commissioner having submitted a report in the above case on motion of Mr. **Moses** for Complainant & consent of Mr. **Graham** Defdts. Solicitor ordered that the said Report be confirmed. It is therefore \ordered/ & Decreed that the said Complainant do recover of said Defendants the amount Reported by the Commissioner to wit the same of four hundred & Ninty three Dollars & [15]/100 with interest on four hundred Dollars from the fifteenth Day February one thousand eight hundred &

Thirty three and that each party pay their own costs and that the order passed on yesterday allowing time to Defendant **John** to answer be superseded the answer having been filed.   **Job Johnston**

The Creditors of **Charles**)
       vs.   )
The Assignees of **Charles**) On motion of **Sims** Complts.

Page 401 _____ _February 1833_
                          February Term 1833

Sol. with Consent of **Wilkins** for Defendants It is ordered that the house & Lot in the Bill mentioned be sold by the Commr. of this Court on some Sale day that the purchase may be paid in two equal installments the 1st instalment to be paid on the first day of January 1834 the other on the 1st January 1835 (purchasers to pay for all necessary papers) with interest upon the purchase money from the Day of Sale Titles not to be Delivered until the purchase money is paid and upon the ~~purch~~ purchasers failure to comply with the terms of Sale by paying punctually at the Day on which the instalments fall Due that the Commissioner resell for cash at the former purchasers risk. It is also ordered that the creditors of **E. W. Charles** do present & prove their Demands before the Commr. of this Court on or before the first day of January next and that said creditors be notified of this order by the publication thereof in the Charleston Mercury twice a month for three months & in three * months [_in margin:_] *this a true copy. It is further ordered that the account of Assignees of said **E. W. Charles** be refered to the Commissioner of this Court and that he report ~~the~~ \on/ the same at the next Court.   **Job Johnston**

Expart **Westley**   )
Freling an Infant) The Commissioner having reported that **Joel C. DuBose** is a fit & proper person to be appointed the Guardian of the Estate of the said Infant It is on motion of Mr. **Ervin** Solicitor for petitioner ordered that said **Joel C. DuBose** be appointed guardian of the Estate of the said Infant upon his giving Bond and good & sufficient Security in the penal sum of Two Thousand Dollars Conditioned for the faithful performance of the trust confided to Him.   **Job Johnston**

Alex Sparks &   )
Coker & **Gregg**)
       vs.   )
Kollock & **Pegues**)
Geo. W. Moye   )
& **J. C. DuBose**   ) On motion of **McIver** Solicitor for Complts. & by Consent ordered that ~~the~~ a Decree pro confesso be given against **Geo. W. Moye** &

February Term 1833

that upon his receiving the amount of his execution entered in the Sheriff office on the 6th Nov. 1830 for Four hundred & thirty Dollars & 14 cents and interest & costs be enjoined from proceeding on his other execution against **James M. Sanders** title the executions of the Complainants are first Satisfied out of the property of the said **Sanders**.   **Job Johnston**

~~Traylor~~ \Taylor/ & McQueen)
   vs.   )
Sarah Pegues & al   ) On motion of **Graham** ordered that the report in the above case as to **William Pegues** & **Pleasant H. Kitterall** ~~be~~ __ be confirmed & made a Decree of this Court.

Jacob Bonds Jun. & others)
   vs.   )
Benj. DuBose & wife   ) The Commr. of this Court having made a report in this case ordered on motion of **Wilkins** that \the/ same be confirmed.   **Job Johnston**

The Heirs at Law of)
A. Yeoman   )
   vs.   ) Bill for Act.
admr. **B. Cosnahan**)
Exors. **D. Mandivill**) On motion of **Robbins** Sol. for Complainants and by consent of **Ervin** for Defendants **D. M. Crossland** It is ordered that the accounts be refered to the Commissioner to report thereon.
                                                        Job Johnston

Elias Whilden[?])
   vs.   ) Bill of Foreclosure
William Dorrell) It appearing to the satisfaction of the Court that the Defendant in this case is ~~about~~ absent from this State it is on motion of **Ervin** & **Robbins** that he come in & plead answer or Demure to the complainant bill within three months from the publication

February Term 1833

hereof or a Decree pro confesso will be given against him also ordered that publication of this order be made in the Cheraw Republican for three Months.   **Job Johnston**

Sarah Stubbs & others   ) +
   vs.   )
Heirs & adms. of **Jos. Stubbs**) It appearing to the Court that **Sarah, John, Ann, Lucinda, Alexander** & **Jackson Stubbs** who are the Infant Children of **John Stubbs** Deceased and **David, Alexander, Elizabeth** & **Margaret Stubbs** who are the Infant Children of **Elias Stubbs** Deceased and **Martha, James, William** the Children of **Alexander Stubbs** Deceased are Infants on motion of **Ervin** & **Robbins** Comps. Sol. ordered that the comssnr. of this Court be appointed the guardian ad Litem & that he do answer compts. Bill.

                           Job Johnston

Same)
   vs.)
Same) It appearing to the Satisfaction of the Court that **Charles W. Smith** one of the Defts. in this case is without the limits of this State is on motion of **Ervin** & **Robbins** ordered that he do appear & plead answer or demure to ~~confes~~ \compts./ Bill within three months from the publication hereof or a Decree pro confesso Will be given against him ordered that the order be published for three months in the Cheraw Republican.

                           Job Johnston

Creditors of **E. W. Charles**)
   vs.   ) Bill for a/c & Sale
The Assignees of   )
E. W. Charles & others   ) On motion of **Sims** It is ordered that the accounts of the Assignees \of **E. W. Charles** be refered to the Commissioner/ to report thereon also ordered that the Commissioner do report the debts Due by **E. W. Charles** to whom due & in what order they are to be paid.

                           Job Johnston

Page 404   _February 1833_
                      February Term 1833

James Hunter Surv.)
of **J.** & **A. Hunter**)
   vs.   )
P. C. Coggeshall &)
Geo. W. Moye   ) On motion of **Sims** and Consent of **Wilkins** for **Moye** & by consent of **Coggeshall** it is ordered that **Geo. W. Moye** do pay to the Complainants the Debts and interest mentioned & that costs of this case on or before the first day of October next <u>an</u> in Default thereof that the Commissioner of this Court do sell the Ho<u>us</u> & Lot in Bill mentioned which **Moye** received in exchange on the first monday of November next with a credit until the first day of January ~~18~~ 1834 on so much of the purchase money as is necessary to pay the Debt interest & costs in this case and on

failure of the purchaser to pay up that amount of the purchase money on said first day of January the Commissioner shall immediately resell for case For the remainder of the purchase money a credit of one & two years with interest to be secured by Bond & good personal security if necessary and mortgage on the Land also that **Peter C. Coggeshall** shall be Discharged from responsibility by making good titles to the purchaser according to the previous provision of the order and ~~it~~ if **Moye** shall pay as ordered then said **Coggeshall** shall make title to **Moye** on said conditions.

Job Johnston

Herbert Hinds) +
& <u>wif</u> & <u>anothers</u>)
  vs.   ) Petition for sale and Accounts
James C. Bellune)
& wife & others   ) On motion ordered that **Geo. W. Dargan** the Commissioner of this Court be appointed Guardian ad Litem for **General Andrew Jackson Hinds, Ann Jane E. Hinds, Ann Stephenson** & **Thomas Stephenson** Infant Defendants in this Petition.   **Job Johnston**

Herbert Hinds)
& wife & another)
  vs.   )

<table>
<tr><td><u>Page 405</u></td><td align="right"><u>February 1833</u></td></tr>
</table>

February Term 1833

James C. Bellune)
& wife & others   ) On motion of **Sims** petitioners Solicitor It is ordered that the Negroes in the petition mentioned be Sold by the Commissioner of this Court on a credit of twelve months except so much as may be necessary to pay the costs of the case that to be cash The purchaser to give Bond & good Security for the purchase money and that the fund be Distributed among the Distribu<u>tes</u> It is also ordered that **Herbert Hinds** guardian of the late **James H. Hinds** do settle his accounts before the Commissioners of this Court.

Job Johnston

Sh. Williams Ordinary)
  vs.   ) Partition & accounts
Sarah Hill et al   ) On motion of **Sims** Complts. Solicitor It is ordered that a writ of Partition Do issue Directed to **James Holloway, Thomas Conn, Hugh Lide, James Lide** & **Thomas Williamson** to divide to the widow her thirds of the real Estate ~~in~~ in the Bill mentioned according to the prayer thereof and that the commr. of this Court on some sale day subsequent to said ~~propert~~ \partition/ sell the remaining Estate both real & personal in the Bill mentioned on the following condition (vis) the real Estate on a credit of one & two years in two equal installments the purchaser to give Bond &

personal security to be approved by the Commissioner with interest upon the purchase money from the day of sale Titles to be executed but not Delivered until the purchase money be paid that in the sale of the personal Estate one third of the purchase

<u>*Page 406*</u>   <u>*February 1833*</u>
                         February Term 1833

Money be paid Down and the remaining Two thirds on a credit of Twelve months from the day of sale with Interest the purchasers to give Bond & personal security to be approved by the Commissioner for the purchase money then the fund arising from the sale of said personal Estat to be held by the Commr. until the complts. account are settled before him and if when settlement thereof the Estate of **Green Hill** Deceased appear to be indebited to the said Complainant then the Commissioner out of the said ~~funds~~ funds is ordered to pay the amount of such Debts to the complainants – It is ordered that the accounts of complainant be refered to the Commissioner of this Court for settlement It is also ordered that the Creditors of **Green Hill** Deceased do on or before the first day of July next present and prove there Demand against the Est. of said **Green Hill** Deceased.   **Job Johnston**

Expart. **Axcey**)
Grice an Idiot) On motion of **Ervin** Solicitor for Petition ordered that after **Wade Grice** shall have executed & Deposited his Bond with security with the Commissioner of this Court that the Commissioner do transfer all the proceeings had in this case to the Commissioner in Equity Marion District to be filed by him in his office and that **Wade Grice** do make acct. annually before the Commissioner of the Court of Equity for Marion District.
                                                           Job Johnston

Joel C. DuBose   ) Bill to examine witnesses and to
      vs.   ) perpetuate Testimony
May M. Mosely & others) On motion of **Sims** It is ordered that the prayer of the Complainants Bill be granted and that the Commissioner of this Court do examine the ~~will~~ witnesses in the Bill mentioned and if either of the Witnesses prayed to be examined should appear to the satisfaction of the Commissioner to be absent from or \beyond the/ limits of this <u>of this</u> state that he examine such Witnesses by Commission.

<u>*Page 407*</u>   <u>*February 1833*</u>
                         February Term 1833

It is also ~~that the Comm~~ ordered that the Commissioner file \said/ ~~such~~ examination with the papers ~~of~~ in this case and that the same to be perpetuated as testimony as by the Bill prayed & that the testimony \so/ ~~to~~

taken by the Commissioner be sealed by him not to be published until the order of the Court.   **Job Johnston**

Jno. B. Bruce admr.)
George Bruce   )
        vs.   ) Bill for sale Land to Marshalling Assets
E. Bruce & others   ) Whereas it having been stated that the Commissioner of this Court at February Court 1831 reported & recommended that the Debts owe by **George Bruce** on his Bond of indemnity to **James ~~Har~~ Hearon** be paid to the Sheriff of Darlington District to be applied towards the payment of said **James Hearons** Bond to the Sheriff and that the said Report having been Confirmed It is on motion of Mr. **Ervin** ordered that it be refered ~~th~~ to the Commissioner to enquire and report the amount of said Bond for which the same was given and who are the persons entitled to receive the same and as to the truth of the above statement.
                                                Job Johnston

Clement D. Wallace & others)
        vs.   ) Bill for Sale and account
E. A. Ellerbe & others   ) The Commissioner having submitted report in this case recommending a sale of the real Estate mentioned in the Bill on motion of Mr. **Blanding** Complainants Solicitor It is ordered that the report be confirmed.   **Job Johnston**

The Exors. of   )
Wm. F. Ellerbe decd.   )
        vs.   ) Bill for Sale & to account
Clement L. Prince & wife)
William T. Ellerbe   )
Alexander R. Ellerbe   )
Thomas R. Ellerbe   ) The Commissioner of this Court having submitted his report recommending sale of the land & slaves mention therein It is __ that the said report be confirmed and that the sa__ made on the terms therein recommended.

Page 408   February 1833
                        February Term 1833

It is further ordered that the Executors accounts be refered to the Commissioner.   **Job Johnston**

James Hunter   )
        vs.   ) Bill for Sale accounts &c.
John Brown & others) The bill having been taken pro confesso as to the adult Defendants & the infant Defendanat having answered by their guardian ad Litem on motion of Mr. **Blanding** complts. Solicitor ordered that the

Commissioner do enquire as to the ~~Respective~~ \necessity/ and propriety of selling all the real Estate and slaves of the Copartnership of **James & Andrew Hunter** for the purpose of paying the debts of the said ~~Complainants~~ copartnership and that matters of account be refered to the Commissioner to report thereon.   **Job Johnston**

Securities of **W. Pouncey**   )
vs.   )
Securities & creditors of same) The Commissioner having reported in this case that the Securities do pay a sum not exceeding Seven thousand Dollars ~~It is on motion~~ the penaly[?] of their Bonds, provided that each Security be required to pay no more than one thousand Dollars It is on motion of **Robbins** ordered that the report be confirmed and that __ said monies or any part ~~of~~ thereof be paid into his ~~hands~~ office that he be authorized to pay the same to each Claimant in proportion to the amount of each respective claim as set forth in the ~~chedule~~ \schedule/ accompanying & making part of said Report.   **Job Johnston**

John B. Bruce admr.)
George Bruce   )
vs.   )
E. Bruce & others) It is ordered that the report and \the/ order leading to it be Dismissed.   **Job Johnston**

<u>*Page 409*</u>   *February/April 1833*
February Term 1833

Exparte **William**   )
H. Cannon Guardian)
of **John J. Cannon**   ) On hearing the Commissioners Report and on motion of **P. C. Coggeshall** Solicitor for **Wm. H. Cannon** ordered that the Commissioner be authorized to give up to the said **Wm. H Cannon** the Bond in his office Due to the Infant by **George W. Moye** and **Wm. L. Moye**.
                                                          Job Johnston

The Court then Adjourned Sine die.

Orders made by the Commr. in vacation.

S. C. Muldrow   )
& **Jno. B. Bruce**   )
Assignees of **B. K. Benton**)
vs.   ) In Equity
B. K. Benton & others   ) It appearing to my ~~Sta~~ Satisfaction that **B. K. Benton** one of the above Defendants is absent from & with out the limits of this State It is ordered that the said **B. K. Benton** do appear & plead answer

or Demur to the Bill of the Complainants within three months after the publication hereof or the same will be taken pro confesso against him – also ordered that ~~Nocit~~ Notice of this order be published in the Cheraw Republican for the space of three months.   **Geo. W. Dargan** C.E.C.D
20 Aprl. 1833

Order made by Chr. **Johnston** at Chancery[?]

S. C. Muldrow   )
& Jno. B. Bruce)
Trustees   )
    vs.   ) Bill for Relief
Isaiah DuBose   )
B. K. Benton &   )
others Creditors)
of **B. K. Benton**) On motion of **Wilkins** for Complainants It is ordered that the Creditors of **B. K. Benton** who were such ~~persons~~ \previous/ to the twentieth day of November ~~with the Commissioner~~ of A. D. 1827 do file and \prove their/ respective Demands with the Commissioner of this Court at . . .

Page 410   _March/June 1833_
February Term 1833

at Darlington Court House on or before the first day of January next under the penalty of being perpetually excluded from any benefit under the assignment of property made by said **Benton** to Complainants.
Signed **Job Johnston**
March 16, 1833

South Carolina)
Cheraw District) I **Geo. W. Dargan** commissioner in Equity for Cheraw District do he<u>a</u>rby ~~comply~~ \certify/ that **Ricks**[?] **B. Wiggins** and **Jonathan Pennywell** were appointed receivers of the Estate of **Mason Lee** decd. but at Feby. Term 1832 the said **Jonathan Pennywell** was Discharged by order of the ~~of the~~ Court of Equity from his receivership and that the said **R. B. Wiggins** has absconded from the <u>Estat</u> of So. Carolina & has been absent for several months & is not expected to return to this state and further ~~in~~ that in my opinion the office of the Estate make it necessary that a rece<u>iv</u>e be appointed.   **Geo. W Dargan**
__ June 1833

The foregoing statement having been submitted to me on motion of **Blanding** solicitor for the Estate of **Mason Lee** Deceased It is ordered that **Geo. W. Dargan** be appointed receiver of the said Estate during absence of **R. B. Wiggins** from this State and that he give security according to law in the same amount which was requested from the other receiver **Pennywill** or **Wiggins**.

June 11, 1833

Henry W. Desaussure

South Carolina   )
Cheraw District) I **Geo. W. Dargan** Commissioner in Equity for Cheraw District do hereby certify that **Ricks B. Wiggins** and **Jonathan Peneywell** <u>wer</u> appointed receiver of the Estate of **Mason Lee** Deceased that at Feb. Term 1832 the said **Jonathan Peneywell** was Discharged by order of Court from this Receivership and that the said **R. B. Wiggins** has ~~ads~~ absconded ~~from~~ from the State of South Carolina & has been absent for several months & is not expected to return to the state and further that in my opinion the office of the

Page 411   _March/June 1833_
February Term 1833

Estate render it necessary that a receiver be appointed.

Signed **Geo. W. Dargan**
June 1833

The foregoing statement having been submitted to me on motion of Mr. **Blanding** Solicitor for the Estate of **Mason Lee** deceased it is ordered that that **George W. Dargan** be appointed receiver of the said Estate During the absence of **R. B. Wiggins** from this State and that he give security according to law in the same amount of which was required from the other receiver June 11th 1833.

Signed **Henry W. Desaussure**

Daniel Myers & others   )
　　vs.   )
Asa Hiram Stewart & wife &   )
another Exrs. **Danl. Myers** others) It appearing that **Asa Hiram Stewart** & wife & **James Myers** Defendants in this case ~~being~~ \are/ absent from & without the limits of this state it is on motion ~~of S~~ ordered that the said **Asa Hiram Stewart** & wife & the said **James M̶ Myers** do appear & plead answer or demur to the Complainants Bill on or before the first day of January next or that in Default thereof the same as ~~the~~ others will be taken pro confesso also ordered that ~~that~~ Notice ~~be~~ of this order be given by publication ~~of~~ in the Pee Dee Gazette ~~hereof~~ twice a month for the space of three months.

George W. Dargan
Commr. in Equity

Sarah Parker et al   )
　　vs.   ) Partition & a/c
Jno. W. Brown et wife et al) It appearing to my satisfaction that **John W. Brown** and **Phebe** his wife Defendants in this case \are/ absent from and

reside without the limits of this ~~Estat~~ State on motion of **Phillips** complainants Sol. It is ordered that the said **John W. Brown** and wife do a̲p̲ear and plead answer or demure to the Bill of the Complainants in three months from this time or the Bill as to them will be taken pro confesso – It is further ordered that a copy of this order be published in the Pee Dee Gazette a public ~~personal~~ \journal/ ~~th~~ twice a month for the space of three months.

George W. Dargan C.E.C.D

Page 412   *January/February 1834*
February Term 1̲8̲3̲3̲

Daniel Myers and others   )
  vs.   ) Bill for partition a/c receiver
Asa Hiram Stewart & wife)
& others Exors. of **Danile**)
Myers decd. & others   ) **James Myers** and **Asa Hiram Stewart** & wife who was absent from & without the limits of the ~~Estate~~ \State/ having by Notice in public gazette been properly made parties to this case & an order pro confesso is ~~rightly~~ \hereby/ made against them It is further ordered that the accounts of the said **James Myers** as Exors. of the said **Daniel Myers** & also the accounts of the said **Asa Hiram Stewart** & wife ~~Zilpah~~ Zilpha be refered to the Commissioner of this Court to report thereon to the next term of this Court – It is also ordered that the Commissioner in Equity be appointed the guardian ad Litem of the Infant Defendants & parties to this Bill.

Geo. W. Dargan C.E.C.D.
8 January 1834

At a Court of Equity holden at Darlington C. Ho. for Cheraw District on 10th day of Feb. 1834 the preceeding order made by the Commissioner since the Last term having been read in open Court were Confirmed.

Henry W. Desaussure
10 Feby. 1834

Page 413   *February 1834*
February Term 1834

At a Court of Equity Commenced to be holden at Darlington C. House for Cheraw District on the 10 Feby. 1834. Present the Honorable Chancellor **Desaussure**.

Expartite   ) Petition for guardian
Thomas Pearce) On motion of **McIver** it is ordered that ~~he enquire~~ it be refered to the Commissioner of this court to enquire what is the amount of the Estate to which ~~the~~ the petitioner is entitled the amount of the Bond to be given by his guardian and whether **Alexander Sparks** is a fit person to be appointed to that trust.

Henry W. Desaussure

Expartite   ) Petition for guardian
Delilah Thomas) On motion of **Wilkins** it is ordered that it be refered to
the Commissioner to enquire into the matters set forth in this petition the
~~account~~ \amount/ of property to which the petitioner is entitled and whether
William King is a proper person to be appointed guardian of the property &
person of the Petition and that he report thereon.

Henry W. Desaussure

Expartite   )
Emily Bacot &) Petition for guardian
Samuel Bacot   ) On motion of **Wilkins** it is ordered that the Commissioner
of this Court enquire into the matters set forth in this Petition The amount of
the property to which the petitioners may be entitled and whether Mrs.
Emily Bacot is a proper person to be appointed the guardian of the person
and property of the petitioners and that he report thereon.

Henry W. Desaussure

Expartite The   ) Reports on Estate & Bonds in his hands+
Commissioner   ) The report having been presented of funds in his hands
ordered to be laid on the table for the examination of the same.

Henry W. Desaussure

Page 414 _____ _February 1834_

February Term 1834

Expartite The   ) Report on Guardians
Commissioner   ) The Commissioner having made his annual report of
guardians who have made their return as also his report on Defaulting
guardians ordered that both reports be laid on the Table for the examination
of the bar.   **Henry W. Desaussure**

Rosanna Lance   )
    vs.   ) Report on Sale
Thomas C. Lance et al) On motion of **Coit** & **Phillips** Sol. of Complainants
it is ordered that the report of the Commissioner of his sales in this case be
confirmed on the purchaser complying with the conditions of the sales.

Henry W. Desaussure

James Ervin adm.   )
    vs.   )
Exors. & Receivers of   )
the Estate of **Mason Lee**) On motion of **Wilkins** it is ordered that the order
pro confesso be set aside and that the Deft. have leave to file an answer plea
or Demurer.   **Henry W. Desaussure**

Daniel Myers & others) amended
    vs.   ) Bill for; Bill for partition & acct.
Asa B. Stewart & wife)
& others   ) On motion of **Sims** it is ordered that the Commissioners report on the accounts of **James Myers** Executor of **Daniel Myers** be confirmed.   **Henry W. Desaussure**

Mary Woods & others   )
    vs.   )
Exors. of **A. B. Woods** & others) On motion of **Wilkins** it is ordered that the Commissioner report on sales of Negroes be confirmed.
        Henry W. Desaussure

J. R. Esterling & wife)
    vs.   )

Page 415   February 1834
                February Term 1834

Wm. L. Poole & wife) On motion of ~~Wilkins~~ **Phillips** Complainants Solicitor it is ordered that it be refered to the Commissioner to ascertain the amt. of rent Due by said **Poole** & wife to Complainants and report the same.
        Henry W. Desaussure

Emily Bacot & others)
    vs.   ) Bill for accounts & partition
admr. & heirs at Law)
of **S. Bacot** Deceased) It appearing to the satisfaction of the Court that **Robert P. Wingate** and **Mary**[?] **S.** his wife two of the Defendants in this case are absent from and without the limits of this State It is on motion of **Wilkins** for the Complainants ordered that the said **Robert P. Wingate** and **Mary S.** his wife ~~ap~~ do plead answer or demure to the Bill within three months from the publication of this order and in Default thereof that the same be confirmed taken pro confesso against them It is further ordered that ~~publication~~ \this order be/ published in the news paper published at Cheraw and one of the Columbia papers twice a month for the space of three months.
        Henry W. Desaussure

Emily Bacot & others)
    vs.   ) Account & Partition
admr. & heirs at Law)
of **Samuel Bacot** decd.) It appearing to the satisfaction of this Court that **Samuel Bacot, Emily Bacot, Peter Bacot, Louisa Bacot, Thomas Bacot,**

Elizabeth Bacot, Caroline Bacot and **Margaret Bacot** Defendant in this case are infant under the age of twenty one years on motion of **Wilkins** it is ordered that the Commissioner of this Court be appointed the guardian ad Litem of the __ minor Defendants & that he __ ~~for~~ them.

Henry W. Desaussure

Exors. **Thomas**)
    vs.   )
P. E. Graves   ) The Commissioner having made his report of sales in this case on motion of ~~Pet~~ **Phillips** Solicitor for Complainants it is ordered that he said report be confirmed.   **Henry W. Desaussure**

February Term 1834

The Creditors of **E. W. Charles**)
    vs.   )
The Assignees of **E. W. Charles**) The Commissioner having made his report of sales in this case it is on motion of **Sims** for Complainants ordered that the same be confirmed.   **Henry W. Desaussure**

S. Williams Ordinary)
    vs.   )
Sarah Hill & others   ) The Commissioner having made his report of sales in this case it is ~~ordered~~ on motion of **Simes** for Complainants ordered that the same be confirmed. The Commissioner also having made his report on the administrator accounts of **S. Williams** ~~& that~~ & that he had paid from the real Estate the bal. Due said **Williams** it is ordered that the same be confirmed.   **Henry W. Desaussure**

Ex partite   )
Peter Bacot   )
Louisa Bacot   )
Elizabeth Bacot) Bill for Guardian
Thomas Bacot   )
Caroline Bacot)
Margaret Bacot) On motion of **Wilkins** it is ordered that the Commissioner of this Court enquire into the matter set forth in this Petition the amount of property to which the petitioners may be entitled and whether Mrs. **Emily Bacot** is a proper person to be appointed the guardian ~~Li ad Litem~~ of ~~th her~~ the persons & property of the petitioners and report thereon.

Henry W. Desaussure

James Hunter Sen. & Exor.)
vs.   )
James Brown & others   ) On motion of **Sims** it is ordered that the
report ~~be confirmed~~ of the Commissioner of the sales of real Estate &
Negroes made in this case be confirmed as to [*crossout*] \John McN__/ &
Shepherd Williams \who have complied/ ~~order was confirmed~~ with the
conditions of the sale and that the report

Page 417   *February 1834*
                    February Term 1834

as to the other purchaser be confirmed when they have compl\ied/~~ainant~~
with the ~~creditors~~ \conditions/ of sale.   **Henry W. Desaussure**

Sarah Parker et al   )
vs.   )
J. W. Brown & wife et al) On motion of **Phillips** Sol. it is ordered that the
Commissioner be appoint the guardian ad Litem of **Nancy Parker** and **William Parker** Infant Defendants in this case.   **Henry W. Desaussure**

Ex partite   )
John Money by)
his next friend   ) On motion of **Moses** Solicitor for ~~pertition~~ \petitioner/ it is
ordered that this petition be refered to the Commissioner that he report upon
the propriety of the ~~appointin~~ appointment and that he do ~~d~~ also report upon
the propriety of ordering the sale and the inactment[?] prayed for.
                                            Henry W. Desaussure

Sarah Parker et al   )
vs.   )
J. W. Brown & wife et al) On motion of **Phillips** Complts. Sol. it is ordered
that it be refered to the Commissioner to enquire whether the contract made
by **Eliza Parker** with **J. W. Brown** & wife two of the Defendants in this case
be for the interest of the Infant heirs of said **Elisha Parker** [*blot*] Decd.
                                            Henry W. Desaussure

Sarah Parker et al   )
vs.   )
J. W. Brown & wife et al) On motion of **Phillips** Sol. for Complainants it is
ordered that a writ of Partition do issue in this case directed to **John Pervis,
Peter L. Robins, Hugh Craig** & **Malcolm Camp\bell/~~lainant ordinary~~** ordering them to Divide the real Estate of **Elisha Parker Sen.** deceased and that
they report to the Court at the next term their proceedings.
                                            Henry W. Desaussure
                                            10 Feby 1834

February Term 1834

Expartite   ) To Guardian
Thomas Pearce) The Commissioner having made his report in this case it
is ordered that the report be confirmed and that **Alexander Sparks** be
appointed the guardian of the Infant petition on his giving Bond & Security
to the Commissioner in double the value of the Estate viz the sum of fourteen
hundred Dollars.   **Henry W. Desaussure**
                                         10 Feby. —

Tho. Stanly admr. of   )
A. Hunter Senr. decd.   )
    vs.   )
Mary Hunter, E. B.   )
Bronson & wife and others) On motion of **Sims** Sol. for Complainants it is
ordered that **Geo. W. Dargan** be appointed the guardian ad Litem ~~of~~ for the
Infant Defendants in this case viz **Solon Hunter, Cambyers[?] Hunter,
Mardem[?] Hunter, Satira Hunter & Mary Hunter** and that he answer for
them.   **Henry W. Desaussure**

Expartit   )
Charles Gee) On motion of **Wilkins** it is ordered that ~~that~~ the Commissioner of this Court do enquire into the matters set forth in this petition what
the amount of property to which the petitioner may be entitled and whether
Joseph B. Nettles is a proper person to be appointed the guardian of the
personal property of the petition and that he report thereon.
                                         Henry W. Desaussure
                                         10 Feby. 1834

The Court then Adjourned.

Tuesday morning Court met pursuant to Adjournment present the Honorable **H. W. Desaussure.**

Exparte   )
Jno. Money by) Petition
Next friend   ) On motion of Mr. **Moses** Solicitor for the petitioner It is
ordered that the report

February Term 1834

of the Commissioner \now/ ~~sh~~ submitted in above petition be confirmed
That said **James** be appointed Guardian of the property of the said **John
Money** upon his entering into Bond in the penal sum of Eight hundred

Dollars that upon his giving said bond he have leave to sell said tract of Land and make in some profitable investments for the Benefit of his ward and that he report what investment he has made of the money and account annually with the Commissioner as to his actings and Doings as Guardian aforesaid.

Henry W. Desaussure

Jno. C. Coit admr.)
    vs.   )
Jona Coit et al   ) On motion of **Coit** ordered that the report of the Commissioner in this case be confirmed the balance in hand of administration being subject to interest \by his/ consent.   **Henry W. Desaussure**

no 3) Expartite   )
Joseph Cosnahan) On motion of Mr. **Graham** It is ordered that it be refered to the Commissioner to ascertain & report whether **Chr. J. Pegues** is a suitable person to be appointed Guardian of **Joseph Cosnahan** and ~~that~~ the probable amount of the Estate to which the said Infant will be entitled.

Henry W. Desaussure

4) Expartite   )
Joseph Cosnahan) On motion of Mr. **Graham** it is ordered that **Chrs. J. Pegues** be appointed Guardian of the person and property of **Joseph Cosnahan** on his giving Bond & Security to the Commissioner in this sum of Eleven thousand Dollars.   **Henry W. Desaussure**

Jno. C. Coit admr.)
    vs.   )
Jona Coit et al   ) On motion of **Phillips** Solicitor for **Jona Coit** ordered that the accounts of **John C. Coit** as administrator of **James Coit** since the last term of this Court be refered to the Commissioner and that he report thereon.   **Henry W. Desaussure**

Page 420   _February 1834_
February Term 1834

Rosanna Lance   )
6) vs.   ) Bill to Marshall Assets
Thomas C. Lance et al) The Commissioner having reported in this case a sale of a house and lot in Cheraw to **Rosanna Troy** for the sum of six hundred Dollars and that this <u>on</u>orable Court having ordered that same sale to be confirmed upon the purchaser complying with the terms thereof It is ~~also~~ on motion of **Phillips** Solicitor ordered that it be ~~eo~~ refered to the Commissioner to investigate and Report what sum if any is Due said **Rosanna Troy** & payable from the funds of the Estate of the intestate.

Henry W. Desaussure

Rosanna Lance   )
7) vs.   )
Thomas C. Lance et al) The Commissioner having reported in this case the
sum of Five hundred and ten $^{95}/_{100}$ Dollars to be Due & payable to **Rosanna**
Troy being the balance of a Judgement Due her & payable from the proceeds
of a house and lot sold by the Commissioner of six hundred Dollars It is on
motion of **Phillips** ordered that the commissioner do execute titles to the
premises to the said **Rosanna Troy** upon her giving the sum of Eighty Nine
Dollars and Ninty five cents the same being the Difference between the amount
of her bid at said sale and the amount Due her as aforesaid.

                                        Henry W. Desaussure

J. R. Easterling)
& wife & al   )
8) vs.   )
Wm. L. Poole)
& wife & others) The Commissioner having Reported that the said **Poole**
and wife are indebted to the said Complainants two hundred Dollars it is
ordered that the said Commissioner do on the first monday in April next
proceed to sell the said house and lot one fourth of the purchase money to be
paid in cash the other three fourths on a credit of twelve months the purchas
giving Bond and security with a mortgage of the premises It is further
ordered that the Commissioner do retain of the proceeds of the sale out of
the share of said **Poole**

Page 421   *February 1834*
                        February Term 1834

and wife the amount reported by him to be Due by said **Pool** and wife.

                                        Henry W. Desaussure

Sarah Parker et al) 9
     vs.   )
J. W. Brown et al) The Commissioner having reported that it is to the
interest of said ~~f~~ infants that the Contract set forth in said Bill of complaint be
confirmed it is ordered ~~ordered~~ that the said contract be confirmed.

                                        Henry W. Desaussure

Isaiah DuBose   ) 10
     vs.   )
Martha Muse et al) On motion of **Phillips** Solicitor for Complainants It is
ordered that it be refered to the Commissioner to ascertain if the facts as set
forth in petitioners petition be true and to report thereon.

                                        Henry W. Desaussure

Executors **Thomas**) 11
   vs.   )
Peter E. Graves   ) On motion of **Phillips** Complainants Solicitor It is ordered that the amount of Sales in above case be credited on the Debt reported to be Due by said **Graves** and that the Bond of **Isaiah DuBose** & **Laurence Prince** the Complainants who were sole purchasers at said sale be Delivered up to them.   **Henry W. Desaussure**

Exparte   )
Samuel Bacot   )
& Emily Bacot) The Petitioners having appeared in Court & chooses Mrs. **Emily Bacot** as their guardian & the said Mrs. **Emily Bacot** appearing & consenting to accept such appointment It is on motion of ~~Phillips~~ **Wilkins** for Petitioners ordered that the report of the Commissioner on this petition be confirmed and that the said Mrs. **Emily Bacot** be appointed guardian of the person and property of Petitioner upon her giving Bond & Security as recommended in his report.   **Henry W. Desaussure**

Page 422 _____ *February 1834*
February Term 1834

Exparte   )
Peter Bacot   )
Louisa Bacot   )
Thomas Bacot   ) Petition for Guardian
Carolin Bacot)
Margaret Bacot) On motion of **Wilkins** It is ordered that the Commissioner report on this ~~case~~ Petition be confirmed and that Mrs. **Emily Bacot** be appointed guardian of the person and property of the Petitioners upon her giving Bond & Security as recommended in said report.
Henry W. Desaussure

Elias Whilden   ) 13
   vs.   )
William Dorrel) Ordered on motion of **Robbins** Complts. Sol. that the original order of publication be extended and that same be published in the Newspaper printed at Cheraw for three months. **Henry W. Desaussure**

Daniel Myers & others) 14
   vs.   )
Asa Hyram Stewart &)
& wife & others   ) On motion of **Sims** It is ordered that a writ of Partition do issue in this case Directed to **Daniel C. McLeod, Saml. L. Dubose** and **John No__**[?] requiring them to Divide the property reported by

the Commissioner constituting the Estate of **Daniel Myers** Deceased equally among the following persons (viz) one portion to **Daniel Myers** one to **William Myers** one to **Erasmus Myers** on to **Patsy Myers** one to — **Mansell** & wife and one to the widow **Zilpha Myers** and make return thereof.

Henry W. Desaussure

Exparte   ) 15
Delilah Thomas   ) On motion of **Wilkins** It is ordered that the report of the Commissioner on this Petition be confirmed and that **William King** be appointed as guardian of the person & property of the Petitioner on

<u>*Page 423*</u>   *February 1834*
February Term 1834

his giving Bond & Security as recommended in his report.

Henry W. Desaussure

Wm. J. Pegues & wife)
    vs.   )
Rebecca A. Irby   )
Adm. & others   ) On motion of **Graham** It is ordered that the Commissioner be appointed guardian ad Litem of **James Irby, Mary Irby, Josiah Irby, Chr. P. Irby, Thomas E. Irby, R. A. Irby, Wm.**[?] **Irby** Infant Defendants in this case with leave to answer.   **Henry W. Desaussure**

Wm. J. Pegues & wife)
    vs.   )
Rebecca A. Irby   )
Adm. & others   ) On motion of **Graham** It is ordered that a writ of Partition do issue in the above case Directed to **Josiah J. Evans, Chr. R. Pegues, James Irby, Charles J. Lide** and **Benj. Rogers** to Divide the intestate Estate ~~agmong~~ amongst the heirs at Law of said **Charles Irby** Deceased and that they make a return to the next Court.   **Henry W. Desaussure**

John Taylor)
    vs.   )
A. E. Prince)
W. F. Ellerbe)
T. R. Ellerbe) On motion of **Coit** It is ordered that it be refered to the Commissioner to examine and Report <u>wheth</u> it be for the interest of the minor **Thomas R. Ellerbe** that the sale in Bill mentioned be confirmed and perfected.   **Henry W. Desaussure**

John Taylor   )
   vs.   )
A. E. Prince   )
Wm. T. Ellerbe)
T. R. Ellerbe   ) On motion of **Coit** Solicitor for Complainant It is ordered that the special report of the

Page 424   February 1834
February Term 1834

the Commissioner in this case be confirmed.   **Henry W. Desaussure**

Ann E. Ellerbe   ) 19
   vs.   )
Geo. T. Hearsey) On motion of **Robbins** ordered that the above <u>cas</u> be reinstated on the Docket and that it be refered to the Commissioner to examine and report upon the accounts of **Wm. H. Robbins** Receiver of the Estate of **D. Robertson**.   **Henry W. Desaussure**

Exparte   )
Joseph Ellerbe) On motion ordered that it be refered to the Commissioner to Examine and report upon the facts stated in the Petition in this case.
                                              Henry W. Desaussure

Assignees of **Furman & Smith**)
   vs.   ) Bill
Timothy D. Pettigrew   )

Timothy D. Pettigrew   )
   vs.   ) Cross Bill
Assignees of **Furman & Smith**) On motion and by Consent of the Solicitors of the respective parties in the above stated case It is ordered that the same be taken up for trial at Chambers in Columbia upon a Report to be submitted by consent.   **Henry W. Desaussure**

In the Matter   ) 22
of **Patsy Myers**) It having been ordered in this case that a writ in the nature of a writ de lunatico enquirendo do issue directed to **Spencer Harrell, Joel C. DuBose, Jno. P. Zimmerman, Sheppard Williams** and **Jesse Clemons** to enquire into the idiocy of **Patsey Myers** and return of said Commissioners having been made stating that said **Patsey Myers** is an Idiot on motion of Mr. **Sims** It is ordered that the Commissioner enquire and report whether **Daniel Myers** is a suitable person to be appointed a committee for said

February Term 1834

Patsey Myers & what amount shall annually be allowed for her maintain-
ance.   **Henry W. Desaussure**

Isaiah DuBose)
    vs.   )
Martha Muse   ) The Commissioner having reported that the facts set forth
in the Complainants petition are true It is on motion of **Phillips** Solicitor
ordered that the Commissioner do execute titles to **Isaiah DuBose** for said
Negroes.   **Henry W. Desaussure**

Samuel Goodwin & others)
    vs.   ) Writ of Partition
L. B. Bright & others   ) The Commissioner appointed to Divide the
real Estate in writ mentioned having made their return and partition It is on
motion of Mr. **Ervin** Solicitor for Complainant ordered that the same Report
be confirmed.   **Henry W. Desaussure**

Wm. McQueen)
    vs.   )
Mary McQueen) On motion ordered that the order for sale in this case be
extended.   **Henry W. Desaussure**

Creditors of **Charles**)
    vs.   )
Assignees of **Charles**) On motion of **Sims** It is ordered that the Report of
the Commissioner in this case be confirmed except that Mr. **McIver** be
allowed to to prove a note before the Commissioner of this court which he
now hold against the said **Charles** which when proved will be entitled to be
paid as the other Demands proved and contained in the Commissioner
Report and that the costs of this suit be paid out of the funds in the hands of
the Assignees.   **Henry W. Desaussure**

February Term 1834

Jennett Hunter   ) 27
& others   )
    vs.   ) Partition & account
adm. and Heirs at   )
Law of **I. H. Hunter**) The Commissioner having heretofore appointed to
divide the property in this case having this day made a further report

Assigning and setting apart the shares of Mrs. **Hunter** in the Negroes of the Estate of **I. H. Hunter** on motion of **Wilkins** it is ordered that the same be confirmed.   **Henry W. Desaussure**

James Hunter   )
    vs.   ) Bill for Sale of real & personal Estate & acct & Partition
James Brown & others) On motion of Mr. **Sims** It is ordered that the proceeds arising from the sale of the ~~proper~~ party made by the Commissioner in this case be applied under the direction of **Jams Hunter** surviving copartner to the extinction of the Debts against the firm of **J.** & **A. Hunter** or so much thereof as may be necessary to satisfy said Debts.
                                              Henry W. Desaussure

In the matter   ) 29
of **Patsy Myers**) On motion of **Sims** It is ordered that the Return of the Commissioner in this case be confirmed.   **Henry W. Desaussure**

T. Stanley Admr. of   ) 30
A. Hunter Senr. Deceased)
    vs.   )
Mary Hunter & al   ) On motion of Mr. **Sims** it is ordered that this case be refered to the Commissioner to enquire into the increase of the Negroes and the unproductiveness of the Lands mentioned in the Bill and Report ther<u>on</u> also to take and report the evidence giving to shew the propriety of granting the prayer of the Bill and if any what ~~property~~ proportion of the Negroes should be hired out.   **Henry W. Desaussure**

Sarah Stubbs   )
    vs.   )
Heirs & admr. of **Jas. Stubbs**)

Page 427   *February 1834*
February Term 1834

Ordered that it be referred to the Commissioner to report upon the accounts ~~admrs~~ of the advancement made to the Defendants.

Exors. of **Wm. F. Ellerbe**)
    vs.   )
Clement L. Prince   )
 & wife & others   ) The Commissioner having Reported Sale of Land and that the purchaser has complied with the terms of sale it is on motion of Mr. **Graham** Ordered that the Report be confirmed.
                                              Henry W. Desaussure

In the matters of   )
Patsey Myers an idiot) On motion of Mr. **Sims** it is Ordered that **Daniel Myers** in consequence of the Report of the Commissioner of this court Recommending him to be appointed the Committee for the idiot and that he do not expend annually more than the profits of the said Idiots Estate also that he make a return annually to the court.   **Henry W. Desaussure**

Exparte   ) Petition for Guardian
Charles Gee) On motion of **Wilkins** it is Ordered that the report of the Commissioner on this Petition be confirmed and that **Joseph B. Nettles** be appointed Guardian of the person and property of the Petitioner upon his giving Bond and security as Recommended in said Report.
          Henry W. Desaussure

D. Myers & others   )
     vs.   )
Asa Hyram Stewart)
          others   ) On motion of **Sims** It is ordered that the return of the Commissioner appointed to make Division of the Estate be confirmed and the Commissioner of this court settle with the parties entitled to receive portions making their portions subject to such demands as may be in hands as received against them respectfully.   **Henry W. Desaussure**

Page 428   _February 1834_
                         February Term 1834

John Irby & wife)
     vs.   ) Bill for Account & Partition
Heirs at Law of   )
Hezekiah Allison)
R. A. W.   ) It having been represented to the court that **Eliza Ann Allison, Caroline Allison, Elisabeth Allison** & **Thomas Allison** four of the Defendants made on the said Bill are infants under the age of twenty one years It is on motion of Mr. **Ervine** Solicitor for the complainant ordered that the Commissioner of this court be appointed the Guardian ad Litum of the said infant Defendants.   **Henry W. Desaussure**

John Irby & wife   )
     vs.   ) Account & Partition
Heirs at Law of **Hezekiah**)
Allison & **R. A. W.**   ) On motion of Mr. **Ervine** Solicitor for Complt. ordered that a writ of partition do issue in this case Directed to Col. **Ben Rogers, Samuel Townsend, James Brown, David Shears** & [_blank_] **Townsend** directing & authorising them to divide and make partition of real &

person estate of the intestate **Hesekiah Allison** and that they make their Returns under their hands & seals to the next court of Equity It is further ordered that the accounts be referred to the Commissioner to report thereon.

Alexander Sparks)
& Coker & Gregg)
  vs.   ) Bill to set aside Judgment & for Relief
Kollock & Pegues)
Geo. W. Moye &)
Joel C. Dubose) Decretal order made by consent see Decree Book.

Exparte   )
John Carloss) On motion of Mr. **Graham** ordered that It be referred to the Commissioner to ascertain and report whether the facts set forth in the Petition be true.   **Henry W. Dessaussure**

<u>*Page 429*</u>   *February 1834*
        February Term 1834+

T. Stanley admr. of)
A. Hunter   )
  vs.   )
Mary Hunter & others) In this case the Commr. having reported that it would be for the interest of the estate that one half of the negroes heretofore employed on the plantation of **A. Hunter Senior** Deceased should be hired out <u>anually</u> by the administrator and that the proceeds should be applied as the will directs the profits of the plantation On motion of **Sims** Complainant Solicitor It is ordered that the administrator do hire out <u>anually</u> at least one half of the Negroes aforesaid and that he apply the proceeds in the manner and to the purpose Directed by the will of **A. Hunter Senr.** Deceased for the application of the profits of the plantation. **Henry W. Dessaussure**

Exparte   )
Thomas G. Sanders)
Samuel D. Sanders) On motion of **Godfrey** It is ordered that the said **Samuel W. Godfrey** be appointed Guardian of the said infants on his giving Bond & security to the Commissioner in the sum of Ten Thousand Dollars.
                Henry W. Dessaussure

Exparte   )
Sarah Cosmahan) On motion of Mr. **Graham** It is ordered that it be referred to the Commissioner to ascertain and Report whether **Cha. J. Pegues** is a suitable person to be appointed Guardian of **Sarah J. Cosmahan** & the amount of the estate of which she is entitled. **Henry W. Dessaussure**

Exparte   )
Sarah Cosmahan) On motion of Mr. **Graham** it is Ordered that **Charles J. Pegues** be appointed Guardian of the property of **Sarah Cosmahan** on his giving Bond and security in the sum of Two thousand Dollars.

Henry W. Dessaussure

Page 430   _February 1834_

February Term 1834

Exparte   )
John Carloss) It appearing to the court by the report of the Commissioner that **William E. Pledger** the Guardian of **John Carloss** never received any property of his said ward and has removed from the State and is desirous to be discharged from this Guardianship It is on motion of **Graham** ordered that the said Guardian be discharged & that his Bond be delivered up to be cancelled.   **Henry W. Dessaussure**

Exparte   )
Robt. Reynolds) On motion of **Graham** ordered that it be referred to the Commissioner to ascertain & Report whether the facts stated in the petition be true.   **Henry W. Dessaussure**

Exparte   )
Robt. Reynolds) It appearing to the court by the report of the Commissioner that **Robert Reynolds** Guardian of his children has removed to Alabama and take his children and their property which is personal with him and that a Bond of three thousand Dollars would cover all the property it is on motion of **Graham** ordered that upon the said **Reynolds** becoming Guardian of his said children in Alabama and giving Bond there for three thousand Dollars & furnishing the commissioner of this court with a complete examplification thereof under the sale of the court and properly certified that the said **Reynolds** be Discharged from his Guardianship here and that his Bond be Delivered up to be cancelled.   **Henry W. Dessaussure**

Exparte   )
Claudius M. Pegues) On motion of Mr. **Graham** it is ordered that it be referred to the Commissioner to ascertain whether the facts set forth in the Petition be true.   **Henry W. Dessaussure**

Page 431   _February 1834_

February Term 1834

Exparte   )
Claudius M. Pegues) It appearing by the Commissioners Report that **Claudius M. Pegues** guardian of **William Allen Pegues** his son has removed

to Alabama and taken his wards with him that the wards Estate consists in personal property of the value of six hundred Dollars and that the property is also in Alabama. it is ordered on motion of Mr. **Graham** that when the said **Claudius M. Pegues** exhibiting to the Commissioner of this court & filing in his office a complete exemplification of a court of competent jurisdiction properly authenticated in the state of Alabama of his appointment here as guardian of his said son and that he has given security there in \a sum/ ~~the same filed~~ ample to secure the wards Estate that he be Discharged from making any further Returns to this Court and that his Bond be Delivered up to be cancelled.   **Henry W. Desaussure**

John Taylor et al   )
    vs.   ) Petition to amend commr. Report
R. B. Wiggins & al) On motion of Mr. **McQueen** Solicitor for Petitioners It is ordered that it be Refered to ~~to~~ Mr. **Graham** in place of Commissioner to enquire and report what sum or sums were paid by the petitioners to **Baker Wiggins** in his life time and ~~n~~ Reported by the Commissioner as ~~having~~ being due **Baker Wiggins** or his Representatives and it is ordered that the petitioner do give security for costs (being nonresident) on or before the coming in of the Report.   **Henry W. Desaussure**

C. J. Pegues & wife)
    vs.   )
E. J. Cosnahan   ) The Commissioners appointed to divide the Estate of **Bartholomew Cosnahan** having Returned to the Court an account of sales made by them of certain of the personal Estate of the said **Cosnahan** and it appearing (in writing) to the Court that the parties in interest all willing the same be ~~eofo~~ confirmed it is therefore

Page 432   *February 1834*
February Term 1834

ordered that the same be confirmed.   **Henry W. Desaussure**

C. J. Pegues & wife)
    vs.   ) Bill
Ed J. Cosnahan   )
Sarah Cosnahan   )
Joseph Cosnahan   ) The Commissioners ~~appearing~~ \appointed/ to divide the real ~~Estate~~ & personal Estate of **Bartholemew Cosnahan** & **Rebecca Cosnahan** having made their Return and Recommended a sale of the Land in Bill mentioned It is on motion of Mr. **McIver** Complts. ~~Solciortor~~ Solicitor ordered and Decreed that the same be confirmed and that the Commissioner of this Court do on the second Monday in March next (first giving public notice) proceed to sell the said Land ~~mentioned~~ on the terms ~~mentioned~~

following (viz) so much as will pay the costs of this suit in cash the balance on a credit of one two & three years with interest fo~~rm~~ the ~~date~~ day of sale The purchasers to give Bond & mortgage of the property and personal security The purchaser to pay for Titles.   **Henry W. Desaussure**

Trustees of **Benton**   )
   vs.   )
Isaiah DuBose & others   )
and the Creditors of **Benton**) on motion of **Wilkins** and with consent of **Isaiah DuBose** & **S. C. Muldrow** it is ordered that **Isaiah DuBose** and **S. C. Muldrow** pay over to the Commissioner of this court by the first day of October next the sum of six hundred Dollars to be by him paid over to the creditors of **B. R. ~~B~~ Benton** who have exhibited and proved their demands before him.   **Henry W. Desaussure**

Exparte The   )
Commissioner   )
in Equity   ) The Commissioner in Equity having filed on the first day of this term his annual

Page 433   _February 1834_
February Term 1834

Report of Estates Bonds & So forth in his hands and the same having been laid on the Table for examination and no objection have been made it is ordered that the same be confirmed.   **Henry W. Desaussure**

Exparte   ) Report on guardian Returns
The Commissioner) The Commissioner having filed is annual ~~on~~ Report on guardian who ~~had~~ have made their regular annual Returns and the same having been laid on the Table for examination It is now ordered that the same be confirmed. It is further ordered that those guardians whose wards are Reported to be of age be discharged from making any further Returns to this Court.   **Henry W. Desaussure**

Expartite   ) Report on Defaulting Guardian
The Commissioner) The Commissioner having filed his annual Reports on certain guardians who are in Default It is ordered that the same guardian who are Reported as in Default in not making th~~er~~ annual Returns as the case Requires be served with \rules/ ~~notes~~ to shew cause by the next Term of this Court why their titles ~~should~~ of Guardianship should not be revoked and they otherwise dealt with as the court may Decree proper It is further ordered that ~~the~~ such guardians as has not given Bond & Security for the faithful performance be ruled to shew cause why the order appointing guardians ~~made not be rescinded~~ should not be rescinded.   **Henry W. Desaussure**

R. B. Campbell)
William Pennywell & others)
    vs.) Report on Sale of Land
R. B. Wiggins & **Jonathan**)
Pennywell and others) Mr. **Wilkins** Sol. for **J. W. Lester** having moved a confirmation of the sales of the land bought at the Commissioners sale by the said **J. W. Lester** and others Mr. **Ervin** Solicitor for Complainant having ~~no~~ moved a resale of the said Land ~~by~~ bought by **J. W. Lester** as aforsaid and the Court having rejected ~~both~~ both motions It is ordered that it be refered to the Commissioner to ~~ascertain~~ examine

Page 434   *February-May 1834*
February Term 1834

And Report to this Court whether **J. W. Lester** was the Real bonafide purchaser of said Land and whether **R. B. Wiggins** was concerned in said purchase as a party.   **Henry W. Desaussure**
                                            12 February 1834

The Court then Adjourned Sine Die.   **Geo. W. Dargan**

                Orders made by the Commissioner in vacation

Jno. B. Bruce &)
S. C. Muldrow Trustees)
B. K. Benton)
    vs.)
Isaiah DuBose & others &)
the Creditors of **B. K. Benton**) On motion of **S. B. Wilkins** it is ordered that to ~~and~~ \Evander/ **R. McIver** be appointed the guardian ad Litem of the Infant Defendants **Lafyeyette Benton** & **Elizabeth Benton** the ~~Petion~~ \children/ of **B. K. Benton**.   **Geo. W. Dargan**
                                            Comm. in Equity
                                            Cheraw District
                                            10 May 1834 —

Emily Bacot & others)
    vs.) Bill for partition - a/c &c
James King admr. **Saml.**)
Bacot Decd. and others) It appearing to my satisfaction that **Arthur P. Wingate** & **Mary** his wife ~~who~~ Defendants in this case who are absent from & without the limits of this state have been advertised twice a month for the ~~p~~ space of three months to appear and plead answer or demure to the Complainants Bill and according to the order of the court and the said absent Defendants not appearing as Required it is ordered that the said Bill as to them be taken pro confesso.   **Henry W. Desaussure**

Same)
vs.   )
Same) On motion of **Wilkins** for complainant It is ordered that a writ of Partition do issue ~~to~~ directed to **William H. Cannon, Robert Ervin, William Wing__, John Fountain** and **William __ Cannon** authorizing

Page 435   _February-June 1834_
February Term 1834

and <u>en</u>quiring thereon a m<u>j</u>ority of these impartially to Divide the real & personal Estate of **Samuel Bacot** that is to say his lands & Negroes so as to allot one third ~~of~~ part thereof to ~~W~~ **Emily Bacot** the widow of the said **Samuel Bacot** <u>an</u> one twelfth of the remaining two thirds to each of ~~his Children~~ the following Children of the said **Samuel Bacot** that is to say **May Wingate, Hannah King, Noah Bacot, Sarah McIver, Emily Ann Bacot, Samuel Bacot, Peter Bacot, Louisa Bacot, Thomas Bacot, Elizabeth Bacot, Caroline Bacot** and **Margaret Bacot** or if the same or any part thereof can not be Divided without injury to the con<u>s</u>erned to Return a Description thereof to this Court with their opinion to that effect.   **Geo. W. Dargan**
2 June 1834

Alexander Sparks)
& Coker & Gregg)
     vs.   ) Bill to set <u>asid</u> Judgment & for Relief
Kolloch & Pegues)
Geo. W. Moye &)
Joel C. DuBose   ) On motion of Mr. **McIver** Solicitor for the Complainants and by Consent of Mr. **Graham** Solicitor for the Defendants It is ordered that the executor **Kolloch** & **Pegues** against **James** ~~Sanders~~ **M. Landers** founded on a Judgment obtained in the court of Common pleas for Darlington District and entered in the Sheriff office for said District on the 25th day of November 1829 for the sum of Two thousand ~~Dollars~~ one hundred and fifth Dollars fifty cents principal & interest six hundred & twenty two Dollars fifty two cents be Returned satisfied and the plaintiff in Execution be ~~forever~~ \enjoined/ from proceeding on the case. It is further ordered that **Joel C. DuBose** one of the above named Defendants and late Sheriff of Darlington District do further pay over to **Kollock & Pegues** or their attorney the sum of one hundred & fifty fo<u>re</u> Dollars & twelve cents to be paid and ~~pa~~ & applied to be ~~pp~~ paid and applied to the full satisfaction of the ballance of an Execution obtained by the Said **Kollock & Pegues** in the Court of Common pleas for Marlborough District for two hundred Dollars in an action ~~fo~~ of business to try title on for [*crossout*] \damage/

February Term 1834

and it having been alledged by the ~~Commisio~~ Complainant in the Bill that the execution standing in the ~~hand~~ \name/ of **George W. Moye** against the said **James M. Sanders** and interned in the sheriff's office for Darlington District on the 13th day of September 1830 for two thousand Dollars ought not be to paid because the Complainants alledged that the said execution is fraudulent and admitted so to be by the said **Moye** and the said **Geo. W. Moye** having neglected to answer ~~p~~ or plead to the said Bill and Decree pro confesso having been extend against him It is ordered ~~that~~ that the said ~~pledge~~ judgment be set aside and ~~Deceased fraudu~~ \deemed fraudulent/ and void and that the said **G. W. Moye** be perpetually enjoined from proceeding on the said execution to collect the said judgment & costs and that said **Joel C. DuBose** having admitted in his answer that he has funds in his hands arising from the sales of **James M. Sanders** ~~to the amount~~ property to the amount of one thousand Eight hundred and Seventy Nine Dollars & fifty cents It is ordered that after deducting the sum of one hundred & seventy five Dollars twelve cents herein before Directed to be paid, he forthwith pay and apply the balance of one thousand seven hundred & fifteen Dollars Eight cents in the following manner the plaintiffs or their attorney in the execution following in the order __ or # stated and to the court stated (vizz)

S. Williams & Co.)	Decree & Int. to 5 Nov. 1831	$35.44
vs.)	Atty. costs. $3 Clk. $ ---	5.00
James M. Sanders)	Shff. on __ —	1.05
)	Sheriffs costs on fifa to be added —	4.85
The State)	Tax $10.80 costs $3.42	$14.22
vs.)	Shffs. costs	2.78
The Same)		
Thomas E. McIver)	on confession & Int. to 5 Nov. 1831	$190.82
vs.)	atty. costs $11 clk. 4.50	15.50
The Same)	Shff. on fifa to be added	8.12
Geo. W. Moye)	confession & Int. to 5 Nov. 1831	$245.85
vs.)	atty. costs $11 clk. $4.50	15.50
The Same)	Shffs. costs on fi fa to be added	9.12

February Term 1834

John F. Wilson)	Confession & Int. to 5 Nov. 1831	$219.39
vs.)	Atty. costs $11. Clk. 4.50	15.50
The Same)	Shff. costs on fi fa to be added	7.17

E. W. Charles)	confession & Int. to 5 Nov. 1831	$110.63
vs.)	Atty. costs $11 Clk. 4.50	15.50
The Same)	Shffs. costs on fi fa to be added	5.02

Coker & Gregg)	confession & Int. to 5 Nov. 1831	$213.30
vs.)	Atty. costs $11 Clk. on 4.50	15.50
The Same)	Shffs. costs on fi fa to be added	7.00

Alexander Sparks)	Confession & Int. to 5 Nov. 1831	$416.20
vs.)	atty. costs $11 Clk. 4.50 —	15.50
The Same)	Shffs. on Exon[?] to be added	9.82

It is further ordered that should <u>the</u> be a balance in his hands after paying those several amounts to be ascertained by the Commissioner he pay the same over to be <u>ap</u>lied to the costs of this suit.

| I have consented to the | Henry W. Desaussure ~~above~~ |
| \above/ Decree **Alexander Graham** Deft. Sol. | A. M. McIver Com. Sol. |

S. Williams)
vs.)
Sarah Hill et al)

South Carolina)
Darlington District) In pursuance of a commission to be directed from the honorable the court of Equity in March last by **Georg W. Dargan** Esqr. Commissioner of said Court We the undersigned have proceeded to examine the land therein named the property of the late **Green Hill** decd. and upon comparing the relative value of the same ~~Record~~ \have/ assigned to **Sarah Hill** \the Widow/[crossout] of the said **Green Hill** that part of the said land designated in the general plat thereof containing one hundred and Nine Acres and numbered 2 and hereunto annexed. In witness wher<u>of</u> we have hereunto set our hand this 1st day of May 1833.

	Hugh Lide
Signed	**James Holloway**
	Thos. Williamson
	Thos. Conn[?]

February Term 1834

Order made by the Commissioner At his office in vacation.

Edward Cosnahan   )
A. J. Miller & wife & others)
    vs.   ) Bill for account & Partition
Danl. M Crossland   )
Philip E. Crossland   )
William Crossland   )
David Crossland & others) It appearing by affidavit that **Samue Crossland, Fernando Lowe** & wife and **Peter M__** are absent from and reside
without the limitts of this State it is on motion of **McIver** Complaints
Solicitor it is ordered that the said **Samuel Crossland, Fernando Lowe** and
wife and **Peter** ~~McIvertyre~~ \McIntyre/ & wife appear and plead answer or
demur to Complainants Bill within three months from the publication
hereafterwise an order pro confesso will be taken as to them and it is further
ordered that this order be published in the Pee Dee gazette for three months.

Geo. W. Dargan
23 Oct. 1834

Alexander Sparks)
Coker & Gregg   )
    vs.   ) Bill for Relief
Kollock & Pegues)
Joel C. DuBose   )
Geo. W. Moye   )
Jas. M. Sanders   ) It appearing by affidavit that **James M. Sanders** one of
the Defendants in the above stated case is absent from and resides without
the limits of this State It is on motion of **McIver** Complainants Solicitor
ordered that the said **James M. Sanders** do appear and plead answer or
demur to the Complainants Bill within three months from the publication
hereof otherwise an order pro confesso will be taken as to tim and It is
further ordered that this order be published in the Pee Dee gazette twice
every month for the space of three months.   **Geo. W. Dargan** C.E.C.D.

23 Oct. 1834

Page 439   *January 1835*

February Term 18<u>34</u>

B. Lilly admr. __)
of **Thomas Lilly**)
    vs.   )
M. E. Lilly   ) on motion of **Wilkins** Complainants Solicitor it is ordered that the Commissioner in Equity by appointed the guardian ad Litem
of the Infant Defendants **M. E. Lilly**.   **Geo. W. Dargan**

9th Jan. 1835

B. Lilly admr. __   )
of **Thomas Lilly** decd.)
    vs.   )
M. E. Lilly   ) on motion of **Wilkins** Complainants Solicitor it is
ordered that a writ of Partition do issue in this case to be directed to **John E.
McKaskill, William Law, __ Bacot, William Wingate** and ~~Caroline~~ \Calvin/
Perkins Requiring them or a majority of them to Divide the Real & personal
Estate of **Thomas Lilly** decd. between **Betsy Lilly** \his widow & **M. E. Lilly** his
child/ assigning in ~~hand~~ such partition one third part thereof to the said
Betsy Lilly & two thirds thereof to the said **M. E. Lilly** and that the said
commissioner do make return of the said writ to this court at its next Term.
                                    Geo. W. Dargan
                                    9th Jan. 1835

Page 440   _February 1835_
                        February Term 1835

At a court of Equity holden at Darlington Court Ho<u>us</u> for the District of
Cheraw Present the Honorable Chancellor **Johnston**. 7 February 1835.

The court having called~~ted~~ upon the Commissioner in Equity & in his annual
report upon guardian & trustees and upon Estates in his hands the
Commissioner submitted ~~to~~ \a/ general report upon the guardians who had~~d~~
regularly made their returns ~~on~~ \also a/ full of the returns with the ~~company~~
necessary comments & explanation one each it is ordered that the same be
~~confirmed~~ laid upon the Table subject to the examination of the Bar and the
further order of the Court   **J. Johnston**

The Commissioner then submitted his annual report upon guardians who
are in Default with their annual returns and also his annual report upon
Estate Bonds & in his hands which reports are ordered to be laid upon Table
~~sud~~ subject to the examination of the ~~cor~~ \bar/ & the further order of the
C<u>or</u>t.

The Commissioner having \then read over in court as by Law ~~reguarded~~
required all the order by him made since the Last Term of this Court which
__ in this journal between the ~~lost on~~ \last term and/ the present it is ordered
that the same be confirmed.   **J. Johnston**

D. & J. Hinds   )
    vs.   ) Bill for account & Partition
H. Hinds & others) **Dawson Hinds** one of the Complainants having died
since the setting of the last Court It is on motion of Mr. **Ervin** Solicitor for
Complainant ordered that he have leave to suggest that fact in the ~~Re~~ Record
& proceed to Reference.   **J. Johnston**

L. & J. Hickson   )
vs.   ) Bill for Relief
C. Clemons   )
R. Frasure & al) The Commissioner having made his Report of the Sale of Lands It is on motion of Mr. \Cervin/ Ervin Complts. Solicitor ordered that the Report be confirmed.   J. Johnston

<u>Page 441</u>   <u>February 1835</u>
                        February Term 1835

Bruce & Muldrow   )
Trustees of B. K. Benton)
vs.   ) Bill
Isaiah DuBose   )
B. K. Benton & others   ) On motion of Wilkins It is ordered that his name be from \this/ time withdrawn from the Records of the above stated case as Solicitor for Complainants S. C. Muldrow and that the mann name of James R. Ervin Esq. be henceforth submitted as Solicitor for S. C. Muldrow.
                                              J. Johnston

C. D. Wallace et al)
vs.   )
E. A. Ellerbe et al) The Commissioner having made a Report of the Sale of a tract of Land called the Belfor[?] tract to Crawford D. Ellerbe for Six thousand Dollars and the terms of Sale being Complied with It is on motion of Graham Solicitor ordered that the Report of the Commissioner be Confirmed.   J. Johnston

C. D. Wallace   )
vs.   )
E. A. Ellerbe   )
Margaret Ellerbe)
& others   ) On motion of Mr. Graham Sol. ordered that it be Refered to the Commissioner to enquire and Report whether it would be for the benefit of the parties in this case to Sell the personal property of the Intestate Thomas F. Ellerbe.   J. Johnston

Francis Mandevill   )
vs.   )
Robert Rogers et ux et al) On motion of Graham Solicitor It is ordered that the Commissioner be appointed Guardian ad Litem for Francis E. Mandevill, Jane Lide & Cornelius Lide Infant Defendants in this case.
                                              J. Johnston

February Term 1835

Christopher J. Pegues)
   & wife)
  vs.   ) Bill for account & Partition
Ed. J. Cosnahan)
Sarah Cosnahan)
Joseph Cosnahan   ) The Commissioner having Reported the Sales of the
Land in Bill mentioned It is on motion of **McIver** Complainants Solicitor
ordered that the Report be confirmed. **J. Johnston**

Nancy Parker)
  vs.   )
Lewis Parker et <u>all</u>) On motion of **Graham** ordered that the Return of the
Commissioner in this case be confirmed. **J. Johnston**

Francis Mandevill)
  vs.   )
Robert Rogers & others) On motion of **Graham** ordered that a writ of Partition do issue in this case Directed to **John McCleanaughan, Robert Ervin, John F. Ervin, P. C. Coggeshall** & **Moses McCall** commanding them to make partition of the Estate of **Cornelius Mandevill** & **John Mandeville** according to the prayer of complainants Bill. **J. Johnston**

J. R. Easterling & ux)
  vs.   )
Wm. L. Poole & ux & al) The Commissioner having made a Report of Sales
in this case It is on motion of **Phillips** Solicitor of Complainants ordered that
the said Report be confirmed. **J. Johnston**

Emily Bacot)
  vs.   ) Bill
Jas. King admr. of)
S. Bacot & others) On motion of **Wilkins** It is ordered

February Term 1835

that the Commissioner of this Court enquire & report what would be the
proper terms of Settlement upon which to Settle the portion of Mrs. **Sarah
McIver** in the Estate of her Deceased Father **Samuel Bacot.**
          J. Johnston

R. B. Wiggins & others)
  vs.   ) Bill or Relief
James Ervin   ) Argument on Demurrer heard in this Case.

S. C. Muldrow & **Jno. B. Bruce**)
  vs.   )
Isaiah DuBose, B. K. Benton & others) Mr. **Ervin** as Solicitor for the Complainants **S. C. Muldrow** having submitted his motion that the said **S. C. Muldrow** should have leave to Dismiss the said Bill as to ~~himself~~ \himself/ It is ~~fu~~ ordered by the c<u>o</u>rt after hearing argument that the said motion be Refused.   **J. Johnston**

The Court then Adjourned to Eleven OClock tomorrow morning.

10 February 1835
The Court met pursuant to its Adjournment.

Francis L. Lee & **Caroline**)
his wife & others   )
  vs.   ) Bill for account & partition
B. N. & **R. F. Rodgers**) On motion of Mr. **Ervin** Complainants Solicitor It is ordered that **George W. Dargan** Commissioner in Equity be appointed the guardian ad Litem of the Infant Defendants.
           J. Johnston

Expartite)
Lewis Stubbs) On motion of **Graham** Solicitor ordered that it be Refered the Commissioner to enquire ~~with~~ whether **Lewis A. J. Stubbs** is a fit person to be appointed trustees and any special circumstances connected therewith.
           J. Johnston

Page 444   *February 1835*
       February Term 1835

Chr. J. Pegues and wife)
  vs.   )
Rebecca Irby admx.)
John Irby and others) Whereas **John Irby** one of the Defendants in this case Departed this Life since the Last setting of this court hearing his ~~and~~ \Widow/ **Ca<u>r</u>therine Irby** and **Sarah Elizabeth Irby** his Infants ~~g~~ Daughter his heirs at Law and **Catherine Irby** and **Robert H. ~~Irby~~** \Mcin/**Tyer** has administered It is on motion of **Ervin** ordered that **R. A. McTyer, Catharine Irby** and **Sarah E. Irby** be made Defendants in this case.
           J. Johnston

Ex partite   )
William F. Asbill   ) Petition for Guardian
Mary E. Asbill   )
Martha Ann Asbill) On motion of **Wilkins** for the petitioners It is ordered that the Commissioner of this Court do enquire into the gross value of the property ~~of~~ \to/ which the petitioners may be entitled especially and whether **William King Jnr.** is a fit ~~person~~ & proper person to be appointed the guardian and that he Report thereon.   **J. Johnston**

J. B. Nettles &   )
Hannah his wife   )
    vs.   )
Charles J. Gee &   )
adm. of **E. Gee** decd.) The Commissioner of this Court having made a Report in this case ~~of~~ on motion of **Wilkins** for Complainants it is ordered that the same be confirmed and that Complainant **Joseph B. Nettles** pay the expence of this proceeding out of the balance Reported to be in his hands and the Commissioner heretofore appointed to Divide the Real & person Estate of **Edmond Gee** Deceased having also made their Return It is further ordered that the amount ~~of~~ Reported by the Commissioner for partition to be due on ~~Dis~~ Division by **Charles J. Gee** to Complainant be paid first by any balance which may be Due him by Complainant **Joseph B. Nettles** under[?] Report of the Commissioner of this Court & next

Page 445   _February 1835_
                       February Term 1835

by the equal proceeds over and above his expences of the Estate allotted to him by the said Return till the same is paid It is further orderd that the Commissioner of this Cort execute Titles to the horses & Lott Referd to in his Report to the Commissioner .   **J. Johnston**

Joseph Johnson)
    vs.   ) Bill for Foreclosure
Richd. Maynard) On motion of **Phillips** Solicitor for the Complainants ordered that the mortgage property Discrided in the Complainants Bill be Sold by the Commissioner of this Court in the Town of Cheraw on the first convenient day after giving Due Notice of the same and that the Commissioner do make report of the same at the next sitting of this Court.
                                          J. Johnston

F. L. Lee & wife & others)
    vs.   ) Bill of a/c & partition
B. N. & **R. F. Rodgers**   ) On motion of Mr. **Ervin** complainants Solicitor and by Consent of Mr. **Dargan** the Guardian ad Litem of the infant Defend-

ants It is ordered that a writ of partition do issue in this case directed to Col. **Benjamin Rogers, Julius Poelnitz**[?], **Francis A. Rodgers, Charles E. Edward & William Cooper** and that they make a Return of this partition and Division under the hands ~~of~~ seals to the next Court of Equity for Cheraw.

J. Johnston

Rosa. Lance admx.   )
   vs.   )
Thomas C. Lance et all) The Commissioner having made his Report in the above Stated Case in Compliance with the order of this Court ordered that the same be confirmed.   **J. Johnston**

Edward J. Cosnahan   )
and others   )
   vs.   )
Daniel Crossland & others) On motion of **McIver** Complainants Solicitor It is ordered that it be refered <u>t</u>to the

February Term 1835

Commissioner of this Court to enquire whether it be for the advantage of the minor & other heirs at Law of **Edward Crossland** to Sell the Real property mentioned ~~Bill~~ in the Bill & that ~~the~~ Report ~~of~~ the Same to this Court.

J. Johnston

Edward J. ~~Crossland~~ \Cosnahan/ & others)
   vs.   )
D. M. Crossland & others   ) It having been Refered to the Commissioner of this Court to enquire whether it would be for the interest of the minor heirs that the Estate both Real and personal Estate of **Edward Crossland** Deceased be sold and he having Reported that it is for the interest of the minor heirs <u>that it is for the interest of the minor heirs</u> that the whole Estate of the said **Edward** be sold it is on motion of **McIver** Complainants Solicitor ordered that \the/ same be confirmed and that the Commissioner of this Court do on some convenient sale day at Marlborough Court ~~Cous~~ House proceed to sell the said Estate on a credit ~~on~~ of one & two years in two equal annual instalments with Inter<u>s</u>t from the day of Sale purchaser giving Bond and personal Security with a mortgage of the property. purchaser to pay for titles so much of the purchase money as will pay the costs of this case to be paid in cash.   **J. Johnston**

C. D. Wallace et al)
   vs.   )
E. A. Ellerbe, M. A.)
Ellerbe et al   ) The Commissioner having made a Report in this case Recommending a Sale of the Negroes of **Jno. F. Ellerbe** It is on motion of Mr. **Graham** ordered that the said Report be confirmed.

                               J. Johnston

Nancy Parker   )
   vs.   )
Lewis Parker et al) On motion of Mr. **Graham** ordered that it be Refered to the Commissioner to ~~ascertain~~

Page 447   _February 1835_
                       February Term 1835

ascertain and Report upon the ⨍ accounts of the Defendants.

                               J. Johnston

N. Hanks   )
   vs.   )
R. Ingram   ) On motion of **Wilkins** It is ordered that the Commissioner do shew ~~case~~ cause why he has not made a report in this case.

                               J. Johnston

Janet Hunter   )
   vs.   )
admr. & heirs of   )
I. H. Hunter & others) The Commissioner hereto<u>for</u> appointed to Divide the Real and personal Estate of [_crossout_] **Isaac**/ **H. Hunter** decd. having this day made a ⨍ further Report whereby they Assign to **Noah A. Bacot** in Equity of his wife **Evanelda**[?] A certain Negroes as his portion of the Negroes of the Estate of **Isaac H. Hunter** on motion of **Wilkins** it is ordered that the same be confirmed It is further ordered that the Commissioner enquire & Report whether it would whether* it would be for the benefit of those interested in the Estate to accept the ~~objection~~ \obligations/ of **Ervin Bronson** instead of those of **Samuel Blackwell** for the land Assigned to **Samuel Blackwell** upon the Division of the Said Estate whether he has yet Executed titles for the said land also that he Report whether he has executed titles to Mrs. **Janet Hunter** for that portion of the Land which has been assigned to her in Division. [_in margin:_] *a true copy

                               J. Johnston

Janet Hunter   )
   vs.   )
admr. & heirs of)
I. H. Hunter   ) The Commissioner having made his Report in Relation to
certain titles to parties of the property in Bill mentioned It is ordered that the
Same be confirmed and that he <u>executitles</u> to **Samuel Blackwell** on com-
pl<u>ainance</u> with the terms of his Report.   **J. Johnston**

Page 448   *February 1835*
February Term 1835

William J. Pegues & wife)
   vs.   )
Rebecca Irby and others) On motion of **Graham** ordered that the Commissioner be appointed guardian ad Litem of **Sarah Elizabeth Irby** an Infant
Defendant in this case.   **J. Johnston**

W. J. Pegues & wife)
   vs.   )
R. A. Irby admx.   )
and others   ) On motion of **Graham** ordered that his name be
Stricken from the proceedings as Solicitor for **John Irby** or his Representative
and that **James R. Ervin** Esq. be substituted in his Stead.
J. Johnston

W. J. Pegues & wife)
   vs.   )
R. A. Irby and others) On motion of **Graham** Solicitor for the Defendants
ordered that the accounts of the Parties be Refered to the Commissioner of
this Court and that he Report there on to the next Court.
J. Johnston

W. J. Pegues & wife)
   vs.   )
Rebecca Irby & others) The Commissioner having made a Return of the
Division of the personal property of **Charles Irby** Deceased it is on motion of
Mr. **Graham** and with consent of **Ervin** Defts. Solicitor ordered that the same
be confirmed. The Commissioner have also reported that the Lands are ~~in comparible~~ \incapable/ of Partition it is on motion of **Graham** ordered that
the Real Estate of the intestate **Charles Irby** be sold by the Commissioner of
this court after having [*crossout*] \duly/ advertized the same in such lotts as
he may believe most ~~adventage~~ advantageous to the parties intestate therein
on a credit of one two & three years with interest from the day <u>o</u> Sale taking
from the purchaser Bonds and Security.   **J. Johnston**

February Term 1835

A. E. Ellerbe and others   )
vs.   )
George F. Hearsey & wife & others) On motion of **Robbins** Solicitor ordered that the Report of the Commissioner ~~be~~ on his final Settlement of the accounts of **W. H. Robbins** Receiver of the Estate of Late **Drury Robertson** be confirmed Except as to the cancelling of the [*unreadable*].
J. Johnston

Janet Hunter   )
vs.   )
admr. and heirs of   )
J. H. Hunter & others) The Commission in Equity having made his Report in this case on the accounts of the administrator It is on motion of **Wilkins** ordered that the same be Confirmed.   **J. Johnston**

James Hunter ~~Junr.~~ \Senr./ & others)
vs.   )
Heirs of **Andrew Hunter**   ) The Complainants having turned over sundry notes bonds & to the Commissioner as part of the fund subject to Division It is ordered that the same be divided among the parties according to their several Rights as set forth in the Bill & answer in such mode as the Commissioner of this court shall Direct By Consent.
J. Johnston

Expartite   )
Wm. F. Asbill   )
Mary E. Asbill   )
Martha Ann Asbill) The Commissioner having made his Report in this Petition It is ordered that the same be confirmed and that **William King Junr.** be appointed the guardian of the person and property of partitioners upon his giving Bond and security in Double the amount of the gross value of the Estate to which each of the petitioners is entitled ~~to~~ as reported by the Commissioner of this Court.   **J. Johnston**

February Term 1835

The Executors of)
W. F. Ellerbe)
vs.   )
C. Prince & wife &)
W. T. Ellerbe et al) The Commissioner having made his report in this case on the Sale of Land It is in motion of **Graham** ordered that it be confirmed.
J. Johnston

Elias Whilden   )

    vs.   )

William Dorrell) On motion of **Ervin** & **Robbins** It is ordered that it be Refered to the Commissioner to ascertain the amount then on the Bond in the Bill mentioned & to Report the same to this Court.

J. Johnston

Emily Bacot   )

    vs.   )

James King   )

Admr. of **S. Bacot**)

Deceased & others) The Commissioner of this Court having Reported the terms of a Settlement advisable to be made in favour of Mrs. **Sarah McIver** one of the Defendants in this case It is on motion of **Wilkins** ordered that the same be confirmed It is further orderd that the Return of the Commissioner to a writ of partition in this case Both as to the Real and personal property be confirmed It is further ordered that the Commissioner of this Court do sell on some convinient Sale day at Darlington Court House all the Real Estate mentioned in the Return of the Commissioner as above except so much thereof as they have allotted to Mrs. **Emily Bacot** widow of **Samuel Bacot** on the credit therein recommended taking mortgage of the property and personal Security from the payment of the purchase money Pearchasers to pay for all the necessary titles It is further ordered that the Commissioner of this Court execute titles to Mrs. **Emily Bacot** in full for the tract of Land assigned to her upon her Complying with the terms of the Returns. It is further ordered \that/ the portion of Mrs. **Sara E. McIver** be returned in the hands of the administrator with the Deed of ~~the~~ Trust to be executed agreeable to the

---

February Term 1835

terms of the Settlement Recommended by the Commissioner of this Court and that so much of the purchase money as may be necessary to pay the costs of this suit be paid in cash.   **J. Johnston**

Expartite   )

Rob F. Rodgers) On motion of **Ervin** Solicitor ordered that it be Refred to the Commissioner ~~of~~ to report on the ~~the~~ propriety of the appointment of **John McQueen** Esqr. as guardian of **Rob F. Rodgers** also to Report the amount of the ~~gross~~ gross value of his real and personal Estate to which the said Infant is entitled.   **J. Johnston**

Expartite   )
Benj. N. Rodgers) On motion of **Ervin** Solicitor ordered that it be Refered to the Commissioner to Report on the propriety of the appointment of **John McQueen** as guard~~idon~~ of **Benjn. N. Rogers** an Infant also to Report the amount of the gross value of the ~~Estate~~ Real and personal Estate to which said infant will be entitled.   **J. Johnston**

Expartite   )
B. N. Rodgers) The Commissioner having Reported that **John McQueen** is a fit and proper person to be appointed the guardian of the person and property of the said Infant and the said Infant petitioner having appeared in court and chosen the said **John McQueen** his guardian It is on motion of Mr. **Ervin** Solicitor for ~~pep~~ petition ordered that the said **John McQueen** be appointed the guardian of the person and property of the Infant upon his giving Bond & Security in double the amount of the gross value of the property of the Infant Reported by the Commissioner for the faithfu<u>ll</u> Discharge of his ~~Jury~~ duty.   **J. Johnston**

Expartite   )
R. N. Rodgers) The Commissioner having Reported that **John McQueen** is a fit and proper person to <u>to</u> be

Page 452   _February 1835_
February Term 1835

to be appointed the guardian of the person ~~at~~ and property of the said Infant \& the said infant/ having ~~appointed~~ \approved/ in consent and having Chosen the said **John McQueen** his guardian It is on motion of ~~of~~ Mr. **Ervin** Solicitor for the petitioner ordered that the said **John McQueen** are appointed the guardian of the said Infant & petitioner upon his entering into Bond & Security conditions for his faithful guardianship in Double the amount of the gross value of the Estate to which __ is entitled to ~~respected~~ \as reported/ by the Commissioner .   **J. Johnston**

Expartite   )
Lewis Stubbs) On motion of **Graham** ordered that the Report of the Commissioner be confirmed and made the order of this Court upon the said **Lewis A. J. Stubbs** giving Bond ~~to be taken~~ and security to be taken and approved by the Commissioner in Double the value of the trust Estate for the faithfu<u>ll</u> Discharge of his duties as trustees The endorsement to be made and Recorded according to Law.   **J. Johnston**

Elias Whilden   )
    vs.   )
William Dorrell) The Commissioner having Reported the su<u>me</u> due on Defend<u>anant</u> Bond It is on motion of **Ervin** & **Robbins** ordered that unless

the Deft. pay the debts & Interest Reported and the costs of this suit before the first day of March next the Land in the Bill mentioned be sold by the Commissioner of this Court to fo<u>r</u>close the mortgage on <u>Som</u> Regular Sale day on a credit of six months from the day of Sale the purchaser giving Bond with good personal security with Int. from the day of Sale so much as is Necessary to pay costs of Suit to be paid in cash.   **J. Johnston**

S. C. Muldrow)
& Jno. B. Bruce)
vs.   )
Isaiah DuBose)
And others   ) The Commissioner in Equity having made his Report in this case in the accounts of

February Term 1835

S. C. Muldrow and **Isaiah DuBose** & the Solicitor of said **S. C. Muldrow** having filed exceptions to the sale it is ordered that the Exceptions be overruled and that the said Report be confirmed and that it ~~order~~ \become/ the order of this Court and that the said **S. C. Muldrow** and **Isaiah DuBose** do pay over the ~~sume~~ Several Sums respectively due by them ~~accounts~~ according to the Recommendation of ~~this several~~ \said/ Report.

J. Johnston

Taylor & McQueen)
vs.   )
Sarah Pegues Exor.)
and others   ) The Commissioner having made his final Report in this case marshalling the whole funds and ~~shevering~~ \shewing/ the Interest of both the Complainants and Defendants therein it is on motion of **Graham** ordered that the Report be confirmed.   **J. Johnston**

C. D. Wallace et al)
vs.   ) [*unreadable*]
E. A. Ellerbe   )
M. Ellerbe et al   ) On motion of **Graham** ordered that it be refered to the Commissioner to enquire into and Report upon the accounts of **C. D. Wallace** administrator of **T. F. Ellerbe** and as guardian of **E. A. Ellerbe** and **M. Ellerbe**.   **J. Johnston**

Expartite The) Report of guardians, Report on Estate Bonds & in his hands
Commissioner) The Commissioner in Equity having Submitted his annual Reports on guardians also his annual ~~Rerp~~ Report on Estates in his hands and the said Report having been laid on the table for the inspection of the bar & the consideration of the Court and no exception having been taken the<u>r</u>to it

is ordered that the same be confirmed and the recommendations therein contained be made the order of the Court. It is also ordered that the Commissioner of this Court ~~be~~ do issue writs against all such guardians as are reported by him to be in default requiring them to shew cause why they have not made the annual return as by ~~said~~ \Law/ ~~en~~required and in Default of such shewing that their

<u>Page 454</u>   <u>February–October 1835</u>
February Term 1835

guardianship be revoked. It is also ordered that the Commissioner do issue Rules against such guardians as have been appointed and have failed to give Bond & Security in obedience to the order of this court Requiring them to shew cause why their orders appointing them guardians should not be rescinded.   **J. Johnston**

The Court then Adjourned Sine Die.

Order made by the commr.

Samuel Goodwin & others)
    vs.   )
L. B. Bright &   )
Jona. Adams   ) On motion ordered that the accounts of the Exors. be Refered to the Commissioner of this Court and that he Report thereon to this Court whenever he should have Examined the same.

George W. Dargan
July 17, 1835

Edw. J. Cosnahan & others)
    vs.   )
Daniel M. Crossland   ) On motion it is ordered that the account of all the parties to this suit be Refered to the commr. of this court and that he Report thereon.   **J. Johnston**

Sarah Stubbs   )
    vs.   ) Bill for account & partition
Heirs and admr. of)
James Stubbs   ) It appearing that **Charles Smith** one of the ~~Defendant~~ parties Defendant in this case is absent & without the limits of this State It is ordered that the said ~~L~~ **Charles M. Smith** do appear <u>an</u> plead ans<u>we</u> or demur to the Bill of the Complainant on or before the first day of Feby. Term next otherwise the Bill as to him ~~the~~ will be taken as Confessed It is further ordered that publication of this order be made twice a month for the space of Three Months.   **Geo. W. Dargan**
28 Oct. 1835

~~Said~~ \Sent/ copy of order to be published in ~~February paper~~ Telescope.
28 Oct. 1835

Page 455 _February 1836_
February Term 1836

At a court of Equity for the District of Cheraw at Darlington held on the 5 Day of Febuary 1836 Present the Honorable **Henry W. Dessaussure**

His Honor the Chancellor having called upon the Commissioner in Equity for his anual reports upon Estates in his hands and upon Guardians & Trustees who had duly & regularly made their return the Commissioner in Equity submitted his report upon estates in his hands also his Reports upon Guardians & Trustees who had duly & regularly made their return and his reports upon Defaulting Guardians (See Report Book) which said reports were by his Honor ordered to be upon the table for the examination of the Bar and for such order as may be taken thereon. **Henry W. Dessaussure**

Jennett Hunter)
   vs.)
Heirs & admr. of)
Isaac Hunter) On motion of **Wilkins** it is ordered that the further Report of the Commissioner in this case be confirmed their being no exception to the Report. **Henry W. Dessaussure**

James Hunter) Bill for sale of real & personal estate
   vs.) & for Account & Partition
James Brown & others) On motion of Mr. **Sims** Complainants Solicitor with the consent of Mr. **Wilkins** Solicitor for the Defendant It is ordered that the report of the commissioner in this case be confirmed.
Henry W. Dessaussure

Chas. Wheldon)
   vs.) Order
William Dorrell) The Commissioner having Reported on sale of the Lands in Bill mentioned It is on motion of **Ervine** & **Robbins** ordered that the same be confirmed. **Henry W. Dessaussure**

Betsey Lilly)
   vs.) Bill for account & Partition
Eliza Lilly) On motion of **Wilkins** it is ordered that the report of the commissioner in this case for the sale of the Land in this case be confirmed.
Henry W. Dessaussure

February Term 1836

Edward J. Cosnahan & others)
vs.   )
Danl. M. Crosland & others   ) The Commissioner having Reported on
sale of the Land & Negroes in Bill mentioned it is on motion of **McIver**
Complainants Solicitor ordered that the same be confirmed.
Henry W. Dessaussure

Joseph Johnson   )
vs.   )
Richard Maywood) The Commissioner having made a Report of sales in
this case it is on motion of **Graham** ordered to be confirmed.
Henry W. Dessaussure

Jessee Clements   )
vs.   )
Geo. B. Mancill   )
Margaret W. Mancill) Petition to recover of the estate of **D. Myers** Dec. the
portion allotted to **Robert** & **Ann Mancille** On motion of **Sims** it is ordered
that the petition be referred to the Commissioner to report upon the facts
there set forth & that he report tomorrow.   **Henry W. Dessaussure**

Emily Bacot   )
vs.   ) Bill for account & Partition
James King admr. of   )
S. Bacot Deceased & the   )
Heirs at Law **Samuel Bacot**) On motion of **Wilkins** & consent of **McIver** it
is ordered that the report of the commissioner in this case on the sales of
Lands in this case be confirmed.   **Henry W. Dessaussure**

Emily Bacot   )
vs.   ) Bill for account & Partition
James King admr.)
& the Heirs at Law)
of **Samuel Bacot**   ) On motion of **Wilkins** & there being no objection made
to the same it is ordered that

February Term 1836

the complainant **Emily Bacot** be authorised to pay over to the Commissioner
of this court all such sums as she may be due the Estate of the said **Samuel**
Bacot Dec. (over & above her share of the same) for the purchase of Land of
the said Estates & that her obligation for payment of the same be then given

up to her to be cancelled. It is further ordered that the money so paid over to the Commissioner be by him put out at interest upon good & sufficient Security Provided that if it shall appear upon making up the Accounts of the administrator of the said Estate that the Debts Due by the said estate Require that money the same or so much as may be necessary for that purpose shall be paid over by the Commissioner to the administrator to be by him used in Discharge & payment of the same.   **Henry W. Dessaussure**

Joseph B. Nettles   )
    vs.   ) Bill for Injunction & Account
J. Gee & W. A. Fraser)
admr. of **E. Gee** Dec.) On motion of **Wilkins** with consent of of **Sims** for Deft. it is ordered that the Defendants in this Bill be Estimated & enjoined from all other proceedings at Law against the complainant in the suit at Law refered to in this Bill & that the matters of account in Bill mentioned be referred to the Commissioner of this court.   **Henry W. Dessaussure**

Jessee Clements   )
    vs.   )
Geo. B. Mancill   )
Margaret Mancill) On motion of **Sims** Solicitor for Petitioner it is ordered that **George W. Dargan** the Commissioner be appointed Guardian ad Litum in the Petition to the minor Defendants **Geo. B. Mancille** & **Margarett Mancille** & attend to their interest in the premises.   **Henry W. Dessaussure**

[*blank*] & **Muldrow**
Trustees of **Benton**
    vs.

Page 458	*February 1836*

February Term 1836

Isaiah Dubose)
and others   ) On motion of **Wilkins** it is Ordered that the report of the Commissioner in this case on the sale of Land in this case be confirmed.
                                             Henry W. Dessaussure

Exparte   )
Isabella E. Hunter) Petition for Guardian
& **Martha E. Hunter**) On motion of **Wilkins** it is Ordered that the matters in the petition Ordered to be referred to the Commissioner of this court & that he enquire what is the amount of property real & personal to which the petitioners aforsaid are entitled & whether **William H. Fraser** is a fit and proper person to be appointed Guardian of the persons and property of the Petitioners.   **Henry W. Dessaussure**

Exparte   )
Isabella Hunter &)
Martha E. Hunter) The Commissioner in Equity having reported in this
case **William H. Fraser** be a fit and proper person to be appointed Guardian
of the infant Petitioners It is Ordered that the said **William H. Fraser** be
appointed the Guardian of the estate of the said infant Petitioners on his
giving Bond & Security to the Commr. in the sum of Fourteen Thousand
Dollars each.   **Henry W. Dessaussure**

The Court then adjourned to 12 Oclock Tomorrow.

The Court met pursuant to Adjournment.

Mary Woods   )
    vs.   ) Partition
Geo. W. Dargan)
Exr. **A. B. Woods**) On motion of **Wilkins** it is Ordered that this case be
continued an that complainant have Liberty to Substitute other Commis-
sioners to execute the writ of partition in this case & that they make their
Return to this court at its next Term.   **Henry W. Dessaussure**

Page 459   _February 1836_
                          February Term 1836

J. C. Coit admr. **Js. Coit**)
    vs.   )
Jona Coit et al   ) On motion of **J. C. Coit** it is Ordered that it be
Referred to the Commissioner to examine & Report upon the Account of **J.
C. Coit** the administrator the situation of the affairs of the estate of the
intestate.   **Henry W. Dessaussure**

Exparte   )
Jonathan Coit)
Guardian   ) On motion Ordered that it be referred to the Commissioner
to enquire and Report whether the said **James H. Coit** is entitled to any estate
and whether the said **Jonathan Coit** shall be excused for making any further
Returns to this court.   **Henry W. Dessaussure**

Thos. Stanley admr.   )
of **A. Hunter Sen.**   )
    vs.   )
) Bill for Sale of Land
Mary Hunter & others) On motion of **Sims** Compt. Solicitor It is ordered
that **Geo. W. Dargan** the Commissioner of this court be appointed the
Guardian Ad Liteum in this case of **Solon Hunter**, **Cambyses**[?] **Hunter**,

Mandana[?] **Hunter** and **Mary Hunter** Infant Defendants to answer for them and attend to their rights.   **Henry W. Dessaussure**

Henry Davis	)
vs.	) Bill for Specific performance of Contract for Sale of Land
S.[?] F. Ervine &	)
others heirs at Law	)
of **Robert Ervine**	) On motion of **Wilkins** it is Ordered that **Geo. Dargan**

be appointed Guardian ad Litum of **Samuel F. Ervine, Elvira Ervine, Sarah Ervine, Lavinia V.[?] Ervine** & **Elizabeth F. Ervine** infant Defendants to this Bill.   **Henry W. Dessaussure**

T. Stanley admr.	)
of **A. Hunter**	)
vs.	) Bill for Sale Real Estate
Mary S. Hunter & others	)

Page 460   *February 1836*

February Term 1836

On motion of **Sims** Complainants Solicitor It is Ordered that this case be referred to the Commissioner and that he Report the credence on this case connected with the fact and prayer of the Bill.   **Henry W. Dessaussure**

Ervin Brunson	)
& **Sara**[?] his wife	)
vs.	) Bill for <u>for</u> accounts Partition & Recy.
Jas. King admr.	)
Samuel Bacot & others	)

ruled twice) On motion of **Wilkins** for complainant It is Ordered that **Geo. W. Dargan** the commissioner be appointed the Guardian ad Litum for the minor Defendants **Solon Hunter, Cambyses**[?] **Hunter, Mandanna Hunter** and **Mary Hunter** in the Bill of complaint mentioned to attend to their rights and interest in this case.   **Henry W. Dessaussure**

Ewd. J. Cosnahan	)
& others	)
vs.	) Bill for Account & Partition

Daniel M. Crossland) The Commissioner having reported upon the accounts <u>they</u> payment of Legacies and the Distribution of the Est. of **Edw. Crossland** it is on motion of **McIver** Compl. Sol. ordered that the same be confirmed reserving the Justice of a settlement for further Discussion.
         Henry W. Dessaussure

Nancy Parker   )
    vs.   )
Lewis Parker &   )
Jessee Bethea   )
admr. and others   ) The Commissioner having made a report on the case and no exception being filed it is on motion of **Graham** Ordered to be confirmed.   **Henry W. Dessaussure**

C. D. Wallace   )
    vs.   )
Eliza & M. A. Ellerbe) The Commissioner having made a Report on the Estate of **Rebecca A. Wallace** and no exception being filed it is on motion of **Graham** Solicitor Ordered that it be confirmed.   **Henry W. Dessaussure**

Page 461   *February 1836*

February Term 1836

Francis L. Lee   )
& wife & others   )
    vs.   )
Beng. N. Rogers)
Robt. F. Rogers   ) On motion of **Ervine** Commissioners Sol. It is ordered that **Geo. Dargan** Commissioner of this court be appointed Guardian ad Litum **Sarah Frances McQueen** an infant Defendant in this case.   **Henry W. Dessaussure**

Francis L. Lee   )
   & others   )
    vs.   ) Bill for Partition & Account
Beng. N. Rogers)
Robt. F .Rogers   ) It appearing to the court that **Sarah F. McQueen** wife of **Jno. McQueen** since the filing of this Bill Departed this life leaving **Sarah Frances McQueen** and the said **Jno. McQueen** her heirs at Law it is on motion of **Ervine** Compl. Solicitor Ordered that the said **Sarah Frances McQueen** be made a party Defendant in this case.   **Henry W. Dessaussure**

Exparte   )
Ann Hinds) Petition for Guardian
a minor   ) On motion of **Sims** it is Ordered that this Petition be referred to the Commissioner to report what Est. the Petition Due **Hinds** is entitled to and whether **Jno. McClenagham** is a suitable person to be entrusted with the Guardianship of her person & estate.   **Henry W. Dessaussure**

Exparte   ) Petition for Guardian
Ann Hinds) The Commissioner to whom was Referred the case to enquire whether **Jno. McLenagham** is a suitable person to be entrusted with the Guardianship of the person & Estate of the Petitioner having reported that this is such on motion of **Sims** It is Ordered that the said **Jno. McLenagham** be appointed Guardian as aforesaid upon his complying

Page 462 _____ _February 1836_
                        February Term 1836

with the usual conditions by giving a Bond in the sum of Five Thousand Dollars.   **Henry W. Dessaussure**

Exparte   )
Emily Hunter   )
    vs.   ) Petition for Guardian
Eleanor Hunter minor) On motion of **Sims** it is Ordered that the Petition be referred to the Commissioner to report to what property the petitioner are entitled to and also whether **Geo. H. Pauley** is a proper person to be entrusted with the guardianship of their persons and Estate.
                                    Henry W. Dessaussure

Exparte   )
Emily Hunter &) Petition for Guardian
Eleanor Hunter) The Commissioner having reported on this Petition that **Geo. H. Pawley** is a suitable person to be entrusted with the guardianship of the Petitioners on motion of **Sims** it is Ordered that the said **G. H. Pawley** be appointed Guardian as aforesaid of the persons and estate of the Petitioners **Emily Hunter** & **Eleanor Hunter** upon his complying with the usual terms by giving Bond to the Commissioner in the sum of Three thousand Dollars in each case.   **Henry W. Dessaussure**

C. D. Wallace & others)
    vs.   )
E. A. Ellerbe &   )
M. A. Ellerbe   ) The Commissioner having Reported the Sales of Land & Negroes in this case It is on motion of **Graham** Ordered to be confirmed. It appearing by the report that **Eliza A.** & **Margaret H. Ellerbe** purchased at said sale the following named Negroes to wit **Charity, Lucy, Zister, John, Isnall**[?]**, Betty** & **David** favorite[?] House servants at reasonable prices that the purchases fell greatly short of the shares of each in said Estate and the Estate is ample the said purchase On motion of **Graham** Solicitor ordered to be confirmed and the purchases be considered as advancement to them for said estate.   **Henry W. Dessaussure**

February Term 1836

Francis L. Lee)
& wife & others)
vs.) Bill for Partition and Account
Beng. N. Rogers)
Robt. F. Rogers) The Commissioner appointed to divide the Estate of **Jno. N. Rogers** having reported it is on motion of **Ervine** Complainants Solicitor Ordered that the same be confirmed. **Henry W. Dessaussure**

Francis L. Lee)
& wife & others)
vs.)
Beng. N. Rogers)
Robt. F. Rogers) The Commissioner appointed in this case to divide Est. of **Jno. Rogers** having by their Report Recomed a Sale of the Real Estate of the said **Jno. Rogers** It is on motion of **Ervine** Complainants Solicitor & by consent of the parties Ordered that the Commissioner of this court do proceed to sell the same at some Regular Sale Day first giving Due & Legal Notice thereof upon such terms as the Commissioner shall deem most advisable for the interest of all the Parties. **Henry W. Dessaussure**

Exparte)
Jno. M. Sanders)
Jas. H. Pearce &) Petition for Change of Trustee
Ann his wife &)
Shep Williams) On motion of **Wilkins** it is Ordered that the matters and things set forth in this Petition be referred to the Commissioner of this court and that he enquire and report whether the Sales of Negroes set forth in the petition by trustee [blank] to wit for the purchase of Land was a good sale for the benefit of the [blank] trust whether a mortgage of the Land Referred to would be ample security for the amount for which the said Negroes sold and whether **S. Williams** is a fit and proper person to be appointed Trustee of said funds with amt. and value of said funds & property. **Henry W. Dessaussure**

February Term 1836

Jessee Clements)
vs.) Petition to [blank] of the Estate of **D. Myers**
Jno. B. Mancill) Dec. the portion alloted to **R. & A. Mancill**
Margarett Mancill) The Commr. to whom this Petition was Referred to report upon the facts set forth in the said petition having Reported that they

are substantially true On motion of **Sims** Solicitor for the petitioner it is Ordered that the prayer of the said Petition be granted and that the Commissioner be authorized to pay over to **Jessee Clements** the Petitioner the share of the Est. of **D. Myers** Decd. that of Darlington District Assigned in the Division of the Estate to **Robt. Mancille** & **Ann Mancille** in right of said **Ann Mancille** and that the report of the Commissioner be confirmed.

Henry W. Dessaussure

Frances Manderville   )
   vs.   )
Robert Rogers admr. & others) On motion of **Graham** Solicitor it is Ordered that the Accounts of the administrator be referred to the Commissioner and that he report thereon at the next term of this court.

Frances Manderville)
   vs.   )
Robert Rogers et al   ) The Commissioner having made a return in this case and no exception filed thereto it is on motion of **Graham** Solicitor Confirmed It is further Ordered that the Commissioner of this court do convey to **Frances Mandeville** Widow all the Lands which were owned by **Cornelius Manderville** at the time of his death Situated in the District of Darlington Marlboro & Marion upon his giving Bond & Security in the sum of two Thousand One Hundred and twenty Dollars to be due in one year with Int. from Date.

Henry W. Dessaussure

Exparte   ) Bill to remove property
Eli H. Lide) On motion of **Sims** it is Ordered that this Petition be referred to the Commissioner to report the facts set forth in the petition and also whether **Eli H. Lide** is a suitable and proper person to be entrusted with the Guardianship of the estate of his children **Frances J. Lide** and **Cornelius M. Lide**.

Henry W. Dessaussure

February Term 1836

Exparte   ) Petition to move property of his children **Frances J. & Cor. M. Lide**
Eli H. Lide) On motion of **Sims** Solicitor for the petitioner It is Ordered that the prayer of the petitioner be granted and that the Commr. receiving satisfactory evidence that **Eli H. Lide** is qualified as Guardian for his minor children **F. J. Lide** & **Cornelius M. Lide** before some competent Tribunal in the State of Alabama and given security According to the Law of Alabaman to double the amount of the value of the property be authorized to deliver to him the Distributive Share of his childrens Estate of their grandfather **Cornelius Manderville** Dec.

Henry W. Dessaussure

Sarah Stubbs & others)
    vs.   ) Bill for Partition & Account
heirs at Law &   )
admr. **Jas. Stubbs**   ) On motion of **Ervine** & **Robbins** Sol. for Complainant It is Ordered that a writ of partition Do issue in this case to be directed to **Jas. C. Thomas, Jos. David**[?], **Henry Easterling, N. B. Thomas** & **Jas. Peterkin** Commanding them or any three of them to divide the real & personal estate of **James Stubbs** amongst his heirs at Law according to their Legal rights and that they report their proceedings to the court at its next term.   **Henry W. Dessaussure**

R. B. Campbell & others)
    vs.   )
B. B. Wiggins   )
J. Pennywell Receiver   )
of Est. **M. Lee**   ) The Commissioner of this court having reported a sale of Land in this case as made to **Jos.**[?] **Lester** but the confirmation thereof having been heretofore resisted by Mr. **Ervine** for those interested it is Ordered now on motion of **Wilkins** with consent of Mr. **Ervine** that the said report of the Commissioner and the sale of Land so Reported be confirmed that the cost of the investigation of this matter to be paid by **Jas. M. Sanders** whose interest herein is Represented by the said **Wilkins**.
          Henry W. Dessaussure

Page 466   *February 1836*
                February Term 1836

Henry Davis   )
    vs.   ) Bill for specific performance of contract
John F. Ervine & others) for Sale of Land
Heirs at Law **Robt.**   )
Ervine Decd.   ) Upon the hearing of this case it is Ordered by the consent of council that the Guardian ad Litum of the infant Defendant do execute and deliver for their good & sufficient Legal Titles for the Land in Bill mentioned [*blank*] farm of the Complainants it is the usual claims of warranty that the Defendant **J. F. Ervine** & **Wm. James** & **Mary** his wife for themselves join in the same and that thereupon the complainant immediately pay over to the admr. of this Estate **Robt. Ervine** Dec. One Thousand Dollars with interest thereon from the first Day of January last and give to the said admr. his Bond in the Penal sum of two thousand Dollars Conditioned for the payment of Five Hundred Dollars with int. thereon from the first day of January Last On the first Day of January next and five Hundred Dollars more with interest thereon from the first day of January last On the first day of January in the year of our Lord One Thousand Eight Hundred and thirty

eight and that the acknowledgement by the said admr. of the Receipt of the money and Bonds so to be paid and given her be a full Discharge to the Complainant for the purchase money of the said Land [*blank*] same shall be secured by the said Bond and that each party pay their own cost.

Henry W. Dessaussure

Exparte   )
C. D. Wallace) It having been Referred to the Commissioner to examine and Report upon the account of **C. D. Wallace** as Guardian of **Eliza** & **M. A. Ellerbe** and he having Reported that the said **C. D. Wallace** was in advance his said wards **Eliza A. Ellerbe** the sum of twenty six Hundred Dollars and fourteen Dollars 70 cents

Page 467   *February 1836*
February Term 1836

and to his said ward **Margaret A. Ellerbe** the Sum of ~~of~~ twenty two hundred and fifty two Dollars 65 cents It is on motion of ~~the Complainants~~ of **Graham** Solicitor for petitioner ordered to be confirmed. **Henry W. Desaussure**

It is further ordered that the Commr. do pay over to the said **C. D. Wallace** the said <u>sumes</u> so reported to be due him by each of his said Ward out of any fund in his hands to which said **E. A.** & **M. A. Ellerbe** are entitled changing the fund of each with the same so paid for her Balance.

Henry W. Desaussure

E. B. Brunson   )
& Lana his wife   )
        vs.   ) Bill for Account & Partition
Jas. King admr. of   )
Saml. Bacot & others) The Commissioner of this Court having made a Report on the account of **Jas. King** Admr. of **Samuel Bacot** late Administrator with the will ~~annet~~ annexed of **Andrew Hunter** dec. It is ~~ordered~~ on motion of **Wilkins** with consent of **Sims** ordered that the same be confirmed.

Henry W. Desaussure

Expart   )
C. J. Pegues) On motion of **Graham** Solicitor ordered that the Commissioner do enquire and Report whether the ward of **C. J. Pegues**, **Sarah Cosnahan** has arrived at full age.   **Henry W. Desaussure**

Expart   )
C. J. Pegues) The Comr. having Reported that **Sarah Cosnahan** has <u>arived</u> at twenty one years of age it is on motion of **Graham** ordered that **C. J. Pegues** her guardian be excused from making further Returns on his pro-

ducing Satisfactory evidence to the commissioner that he has fully settled with his ward.　　　　　　　　　　　**Henry W. Desaussure**

Betsey Lilly admx.)
　　vs.　　　　　　)
Mary Lilly　　　) The Commissioner appointed to <u>divid</u> Estate of **Thos. Lilly** dec. having made the Return

Page 468　　　　　　　　　　　　　　　　　　_February 1836_
February Term 1836

It is on motion of **Wilkins** Complainant Solicitor ordered that it be ~~refered~~ Confirmed.　　　　　　　　　　　　**Henry W. Desaussure**

Expartite **James Law**) Petition to substitute Trustees
& **M. L. Pettigrew**　) On motion of **Sims** it is ordered that this petition be Refered to ~~to~~ the Commissioner to Report upon the amount ~~amount~~ of the trust funds mentioned in the Petition.　　**Henry W. Desaussure**

The Court then adjourned to 10 oclock Wednesday Morning.

The Court met Pursuant to Adjournment.

Expartite　　　　　　)
The Commissioner) The Commissioner in Equity having <u>Red</u> to the Court all the orders made by him since the last Term of this Court that there being no objection thereto it is ordered by the Court that the said order be confirmed.　　　　　　　　　　　**Henry W. Desaussure**

Expartite The　　　　　) Report on Estate &c.
Commissioner in Equity) The Report of the Commissioner in Equity & having been made on the first day of this Court and no objection having been made there to it is by the Court ordered to be confirmed.
　　　　　　　　　　　　　　　Henry W. Desaussure

Expartite　　) Report of the commr. on guardian
The Commr.) who have duly made their returns
The Commissioner having made his Report on those guardians who have duly & regularly made their return to and no objection being made it is ordered that the Same be Confirmed.　　**Henry W. Dessausure**

Expartite　　) Report on defaulting Guardian
The Commr.) The Commissioner having submitted his Report on defaulting guardians and the same \having been/ ~~be given~~ laid __ for consideration it is ~~ord~~ now ordered that

February Term 1836

that such Guardians as were at the last term Reported to be in default with \their annual/ ~~receiver~~ Returns but who have since that time made satisfactory Returns to the Commissioner be discharged from the rules ordered against them on their paying up all costs incurred, in consequences of their ~~several~~ \several/ Defaults It is further ordered that the appointment of Mrs. **Emily Bacot** as the guardian of \her/ Eight Infant Children be rescinded to that the said Mrs. **Bacot** pay all the costs attended upon her appointment as guardian and the Rule against her for ~~complainants~~ \noncompliance/ with the condition ~~of~~ of the said appointment It is further ordered that the appointment of **Daniel Myers** as the Trustee of **Patsy Myers** an Idiot be recinded he having failed to qualify his by giving the Bond and Security Required & that he pay the costs of appointment For the same reason it is ordered that the appointment of **Joel C. DuBose** as guardian of **Frances Benett** be ~~rescinded~~ rescinded.   **Henry W. Desaussure**

It is ordered **James Gillispie** guardian of **Julia M. Hawes** and **Martha Williams** guardian of **Harriet Williams** be Discharged from making further Returns it appearing that their several wards are of age or married It is further ordered that all the guardians & Trustees who are Reported as being in Default in not having made their annual Returns \be/ served with the usual ~~writs~~ \rules/ to be issured by the Commissioner. It is further ordered that all such persons as have been appointed guardians and Trustees & have not given Bond & Security be served with a rule to ~~them~~ shew cause why their appointment shall not be rescinded.   **Henry W. Desaussure**

Expartite **Jno.**   )
Coit guardian   )
of **James H. Coit**) The Commissioner having Reported in this case that **James H. Coit** the Infant has received no property from his father's Estate the said Estate being insolvent and that the said **Jno. Coit** be excused from making further Returns as guardian it is on motion of **Coit** ordered that the said Report be Confirmed & that said guardian be excused from making further Returns.   **Henry W. Desaussure**

February Term 1836

Jno. C. Coit admr.   )
of **Jas. Coit**   )
    vs.   )
Jona. Coit and others) The Commissioner having made his final Report ~~Report~~ upon the accounts of **John C. Coit** admr. of **Jas. Coit** it is ordered that the ~~the~~ ~~Said~~ Same be Confirmed.   **Henry W. Desaussure**

S. C. Muldrow &   )
Jno. B. Bruce   )
   vs.   )
Isaiah DuBose et al) It appearing that the Costs of Mr. **Moses** Solicitor for one of the creditors in this contract by the Commr. at fifteen Dollars was not paid out of the funds already in the hands of the Commissioner and which funds are otherwise appointed it is ordered that the Commissioner do pay the said costs out of the pr͟ceeds of the Bond taken ~~out of~~ from the sale of the land when collected.   **Henry W. Desaussure**

Expartite   ) Petition for the ~~Petition~~ \Substitution/ of trustee
James Lane &   )
Martha L. Pettigrew) The Commissioner in Equity to whom this petition was Refered to enquire of the facts Set forth therein and also as to the amount of the Trust property mentioned having made his Report On motion of **Sims** Solicitor for petitioner It is further ordered that ~~the~~ \in/ accordance with the prayer of the petitioner **George W. Dargan** Commissioner in Equity be ~~submitted~~ \Substituted/ in the place of **John B. Bruce** the former trustee under ~~the age~~ the will of **Racheal**[?] **Lane** decd. upon his giving Bond & Security for the faithful performance of his trust in the penal sum of forty Thousand Dollars and Report the same to the next court.
                                                      Henry W. Desaussure

Tho. Stanley admr.   )
of **A. Hunter**   )
   vs.   )
Mary Hunter & others) ~~The Comm~~ This case having been

Page 471   *February 1836*
February Term 1836

Refered to the Commissioner of this Court ~~cort~~ to Report upon the facts of the case and he ~~being~~ \having/ Reported thereon on motion of **Sims** Complainants Solicitor It is ordered that the Commissioner [*crossout*] \on some/ sale having given legal notice thereof do sell the following ~~account~~ land belonging to the Real Estate of **Andrew Hunter Sen.** deceased __ a tract of Land called the mill tract another tract of Land called the Dusty Hill Tract other ~~several~~ tract another called Hickory Hill and also one other several tract containing one hundred acres near the ~~landing~~ lands of **James R. Ervin** on High Hill on the following terms the purchasers to pay one fo͟rth of the purchase money in cash & the balance in two equal annual inst͟alments on one and two years credit~~ed~~ with interest on the same day of sale the purchaser giving Satisfactory Security to the Commissioner for the same. It is further ordered that upon the purchasers complying with the terms of sale the Commissioner is authorized to execute ~~th~~ titles to them for the said lands and to turn over the cash and Bond for the purch͟as ~~req~~ ~~p~~ money to **Thomas Stanly** administrator of **A. Hunter** decd. to be \used by/ ~~made by~~ him in the settlement of his testators Debts and to pay the necessary exp<u>ece</u>s of the Estate It is also ordered that the Report of the Commissioner be confirmed.

Henry W. Desaussure

Edward J. Cosnahan & others)
    vs.   )
Daniel M. Crossland & others) On motion ~~Du~~ of **Dudly** Soli. for the said **Elizabeth Grant** ordered that it be Refe<u>re</u>d \back/ to the Commissioner to enquire into & Report upon the propriety of ~~Conying~~ \conveying/ to a proper Trustee the interest of the said **Elizabeth Grant** in the Estate of the said **Edward Crossland** for the Sole and ~~exact~~ \sep<u>e</u>rate/ use of the said **Elizabeth Grant**.

Henry W. Desaussure

Expartite)
Joshua M. Sanders) Petition for change of Trustees & <u>soforthe</u>
James H. Pearce)
& **Ann** his wife &)
Shepherd Williams) The Commissioner having Reported favorably on the facts set forth in the petition

---

Page 472   *February 1836*

February Term 1836

It is ~~ordered that~~ ordered on motion of **Wilkins** that **Sheppard Williams** be appointed trustee of the property Refered to in said petition upon his giving Bond with good Security to be taken by the Commissioner in Double the ~~valen~~ value of the said property conditioned for the faithful d<u>i</u>charge of the Duties of the trust that \the/ upon the property be Delivered ~~to~~ up to him and upon settl<u>m</u>ent with the ~~the~~ former trustee **Joshua M. Sanders** should be authorized to give to the said **Joshua** __ on Discharge for the same and upon the said **James H. Pearce** executing a mortgage to **Sheppard Williams** of the land Refe<u>r</u>d to for the security of his payment of the purchase money of the Negroes sold the sale be confirmed and the said **Joshua M.** thence__ and Discharged from all Duties and Liabilities as trustee as aforesaid.

Henry W. Desaussure

Nathan Hanks)
    vs.   )
Richard Ingram) This case heard before the chancellors on exception to the commissioner Report.   **Henry W. Desaussure**

E. B. Brunson & wife)
    vs.   )
Jas. King admr. of   )
Sam Bacot & others   ) This case heard before the Chancellors on Bill and answer.

The Court <u>the</u> Adjourned to 9 oclock To morrow morning.

The Court met pursuant to Adjournment.

Expartite **Clement**)
C. D. Wallace   ) On motion of **Graham** Solicitor it is ordered that the Commissioner do enquire and Report whether **William Kervin** the security of **C. D. Wallace** as guardian of **E. A. Ellerbe** and **M. A. Ellerbe** has Removed

<u>Page 473</u>   <u>February 1836</u>
                              February Term 1836

from this State and whether the said **Wallace** as any Estate of either of his said ward in his hands.   **Henry W. Desaussure**

Expartite   )
C. D. Wallace) The Commissioner of this Court having Reported that **William Kirven** one of the securities of **C. D. Wallace** as guardian of **Eliza A. Ellerbe** and **Margaret A. Ellerbe** has Removed from the state and that the said [*crossout*] **Wallace**/ has at this time no Estate of either of his ~~hands~~ \wards/ **E. A. Ellerbe** and **M. A. Ellerbe** in his hands & that each ones ~~time~~ \heirs/ at this time a considerable balance and that \the/ above Estate of said wards is at this time in the hands of the commissioner It is on motion of **Graham** Solicitor ordered that the bond heretofore given by **C. D. Wallace** as guardian of **Eliza A. Ellerbe** and **Margaret A. Ellerbe** to which **William Kervin** as security be delivered ~~to the~~ up to be cancelled on said **Wallace** giving Bond & security ~~and~~ \as/ guardian of Each of his said wards to be approved by the Commissioner in the sum of thirty thousand Dollars each.
                                    Henry W. Desaussure

Expartite   )
James Gillispie)
Guardian of   )
M. J. Hanes   ) On motion of **Graham** Solicitor pro petr. it is ordered that it Refered to the Commissioner to enquire and Report whether **M. J. Hanes** has ~~maintain~~ \arrived/ at the age of twenty one years and whether **James Gillispie** has settled with her as guardian.   **Henry W. Desaussure**

Expartite   )
James Gillispie)
Guardian   ) It having been Refered to the Commissioner to enquire and Report whether **M. J. Hanes** has arrived <u>arrived</u> at full age and whether **James Gillispie** his Guardian has settled ~~if~~ in full with his said ward and that

Page 474   *February 1836*
February Term 1836

the Commissioner having Reported that the <u>he</u> has arrived at the age of twenty one years and that the said **Gillispe** has settled with her in full on motion of **Graham** it is ordered that the said Report be confirmed. It is further ordered that the said **Gillispie** be excused from making any further Returns and that his Bond as guardian \be/ cancelled.

Henry W. Desaussure

Expartite   )
Thom. S. Wallace) Petition for guardian
by his next friend   )
C. D. Wallace   ) The Commissioner having Reported that **Clement D. Wallace** is a suitable person to be appointed the guardian of his son **Thomas S. Wallace** and that his Estate amounts to something ~~that the said Clement D. Wallace~~ less than four thousand Dollars it is ordered that the said **Clement D. Wallace** be appointed guardian of the Estate of his Son **Thomas S. Wallace** on his giving Bond and Security to be approve by the commissioner in the sum of Eight thousand Dollars.   **Henry W. Desaussure**

Expartite   )
W. D. Wallace   )
by his next friend)
C. D. Wallace   ) On motion of **Graham** Solicitor ordered that the Commissioner enquire and Report ~~weth~~ whether **Clement D. Wallace** is a suitable person to be appointed guardian of his Infant son **William D. Wallace** and the amount of the Estate to which the Said **William D. Wallace** is entitled.

Henry W. Desaussure

Expartite   )
W. D. Wallace   )
by his next friend)
C. D. Wallace   ) The Commissioner having Reported that **Clement D. Wallace** is a suitable person to be appointed guardian of the Estate of his son

Page 475   *February 1836*
February Term 1836

William D. Wallace and that his Estate amount to something short of four thousand Dollars it is ordered that the said **C. D. Wallace** be appointed the guardian of the Estate of his said Son **William D. Wallace** on his giving Bond and security to be approved by the commissioner in the <u>sume</u> of Eight thousand Dollars.   **Henry W. Desaussure**

Edward J. Cosnahan   )
and others   )
        vs.   ) Bill for Partition & Account
Daniel M. Crossland & others) It having been Refered to the Commissioner to enquire into and Report upon the terms of Settlement to be made
upon **Elizabeth** the wife of **Richard S. Grant** of all his ~~action~~ \interest/ in the
Estate of **Edward Crossland** Deceased and the Commissioner ~~have~~ \having/
made a Report It is ordered that it be Refered again to the Commissioner to
have additional evidence and report upon the ter_mes_ of Settlement to be
made on the said **Elizabeth Grant** at the next term of this Court.
                                          Henry W. Desaussure

E. B. Brunson & wife)
        vs.   )
James King admr.   )
of **S. Bacot** & others) The argument of this case was resumed & concluded.

Expartite   )
C. D. Wallace   ) Bill for an order for allowance
guardian of   )
Eliza A. Ellerbe &)
Margarat A. Ellerbe) On hearing this petition it is ordered that it be refered
to the Commissioner to enquire & Report what sum it could be proper to
allow to the said **E. A. Ellerbe** and **M. M. Ellerbe** annually for their main-
ta_i_nance and S_pp_ort.   **Henry W. Desaussure**

Expartite   )
C. D. Wallace) Petition for allowance for wards
guardian   ) (turn over)

February Term 1836

Eliza A. Ellerbe and)
Margaret A. Ellerbe) It having been Refered to the Commissioner to
enquire and report what would be a proper annual allowance for the main-
ta_i_nance & Support of the Said ~~Estate~~ **E. A. Ellerbe** and **M. A. Ellerbe** & he
having reported that upon considering the amount of the Estate of the said
Wards he recommends the sum of five hundred Dollars to be allowed each of
them. It is on motion ordered the said report be confirmed & the recommendation _theof_ become the order of this court.
                                          Henry W. Desaussure

Expartite   )
C. D. Wallace guardian)
Eliza A. Ellerbe   ) ~~Bill~~
M. A. Ellerbe   ) Petition to account[?] funds of ward
William ~~D~~ Wallace)
Thomas S. Wallace) On motion of **Graham** it is ordered that it be refered to the Commissioner to enquire and Report <u>wheth</u> it would be expedient and proper & for the ~~Estate~~ interest of the Infant ward of the said **C. D. Wallace** to <u>inrust</u> the funds now in the hands of the Commissioner arising from the Sale of the Estate of **Thomas ~~E~~ F. Ellerbe** in bank stock or in some other safe and ~~property~~ \profitable/ investment.

              Henry W. Desaussure

Expartite **C. D. Wallace**)
guardian of **E. A. Ellerbe**)
M. A. Ellerbe, W. D.   )
Wallace & Thos. S. Wallace) It having been referred to the Commissioner of this court to enquire into the expedience of investing the funds of the said wards in Bank Stock or in some other ~~property~~ \profitable investment/ ~~and that~~ and the commissioner having made his report it is ~~orderd~~ ordered that the same be confirmed ~~and th~~ & that the recommendation thereof be made the order of the court but the Commissioner is specially charged to be ~~g~~ very guarded in such investment & not to act or make such investment settlement having proper<u>ll</u>y satisfied that it is a safe as made as beneficial investment.

              Henry W. Desaussure

Page 477   *August 1836*
       February Term 1836

Samuel[?] **Sellars** & others)
  vs.   ) In Equity
John Evans, Turner ~~B~~)
Bryan, John Sellars & others) It appearing to the Satisfaction of the Court that **John Sellars, Richard Sellars, Thomas Gaddy**[?] & **Mary** his wife **Elijah ~~Gee Eage~~ Eullage** and **Phebe Eullage** Defendants in the above stated case are absent from and ~~reid~~ \reside/ without the limits of this state It is on motion of **Robbins** and **McIver** Complainants Solicitor ordered that the said <u>Defants</u> do appear and plead answer or demure to the complainants Bill within three months after the publication of this order or a Decree pro confesso will be taken against them. It is further ordered that the order be published twice a month for the space of three months in the Cheraw Gazette.

              Geo W. Dargan
22 Aug. 1836   Commr. in Equity C. D.

January Term 1837

At a Court of Equity for the District of Cheraw at Darlington held on the 9th day of January 1837 Present the Honorable **Wm. Harper**.

His Honour the Chancellor having called upon the Commissioner in Equity for his annual Report upon Estate in his hands and upon Guardians and Trustees the Commissioner submitted his Report upon Estates in his hands also his Reports upon Guardian and Trustees who had Duly made Regularly made their Returns and his Report upon Defaulting Guardians (See Report Book) which said Reports were by his Honour ordered to be on the table for the examination of the Bar and for such orders as may be taken thereon.
                                                                    Wm. Harper

Exparte   )
Joseph Cosnahan) On motion of **Graham** ordered that it be Refered to the Commissioner to enquire and Report whether Dr. **William Crosland** is a suitable person to be appointed Guardian of **Joseph Cosnahan** instead of **Ch**[*blot*] **J. Pegues** his former guardian.

Exparte   )
Joseph Cosnahan) The Commissioner having reported it is ordered that the Report be confirmed and that **William Crosland** be appointed guardian of **Joseph Cosnahan** upon his giving Bond & Security ~~to Sta~~ Satisfactory to the Commissioner in the amount given by the late guardian **Ch**[*blot*] **J. Pegues** and the guardianship of **Christopher J. Pegues** ~~see~~ be Revoked.

Exparte   ) Petition for Guardianship
Elias Windham) On motion of Solicitor for the Petition It is ordered that this petition be Referred to the Commissioner to Report on the facts of the petition and whether **Elias Windham** is a proper person to be entrusted with the guardianship of his son's Estate and if ~~so much~~ so for what amount his should ~~be~~ give Bond.   **W. Harper**

January Term 1837

Exparte   ) Petition for Guardian
Sarah A. Conner   )
Edward G. Conner) On motion of **Sims** Solicitor for the Petitioners it is ordered that this Petition be Refered to the Commissioner to Report on the facts stated in the Petition and whether **Edmund Mancile** is a fit and proper person to be entrusted with the guardianship of **Sarah A. Conner** and **Edmund Conner** also in what amount he should give Security.
                                                                    W. Harper

Wm. McQueen   )

vs.   )

Mary McQueen et al) On motion of **Graham** Solicitor ordered that the order of sale in this case be extended.   **Wm. Harper**

The Executors of)

Wm. F. Ellerbe   )

vs.   )

C. Prince & wife) The Commissioner having made a report in this case on motion of **Graham** ~~it ref~~ it is approved. It is further ordered that **W. T. Ellerbe** do shew cause to the commissioner of this court on or before the first day June next why he has not complyed with the term of the sale made on 23 Jany. 1835 last.   **Wm. Harper**

Francis L. Lee & others   )

vs.   ) Bill for Account & Partition

B. N. Rogers   )

Robert F. Rogers   ) The Commissioner having reported on the Accounts of the Administrator it is on motion of **Robbins** & **McIver** ordered that the same be confirmed.   **Wm. Harper**

Joseph Melton   )

vs.   )

Thomas Sims[?]) It appearing by the Complainant Bill that he Resides in the county of Anson in the state of North Carolina

Page 480 _____ _January 1837_

January Term 1837

North Carolina It is on motion of **Graham** Solicitor for Defendant ordered that the Complainants give Security for the costs of this ~~cas~~ suit on satisfactory to the Commissioner on or before the first day of July next or that the Bill be ~~Discharg~~ Dismissed with costs.   **Wm. Harper**

Thomas Stanly admr.)

of **A. Hunter Sr.**   )

vs.   )

Mary Hunter et al   ) The Commissioner having made a report in this case it is ordered that he report be confirmed as to the purchase of **W. H. Cannon** and that the sale to **Jas. Hunter** be confirmed when he complies with the conditions of sale. It is further ordered that the ~~person~~ \previous/ order made in this case so far as not executed be executed.   **Wm. Harper**

Janet Hunter   )
vs.   )
Admr. & Heirs)
of **J. H. Hunter**) The Commissioner having Reported in this case it is on motion of **Wilkins** Solicitor ordered that said Report be confirmed.
                              Wm. <u>Hunter</u>

Jas. Hunter   )
vs.   )
Legatees of **A. Hunter Sr.**) The Commissioner having made his Report in this case on motion of **Sim<u>e</u>s** it is ordered that that the Report be confirmed.
                              Wm. Harper

Levina Sellars   )
Hard<u>a</u>y H. Sellars)
Zylpha A. Sellars)
vs.   )
John Evans   )
Turner B. Evans   )
John Sellars &   )
  others   ) On motion of **Robbins** & **McIver** Complainants Solicitor It is ordered that a writ of

Page 481   *January 1837*
                         January Term 1837

of Partition in this case do issue ~~in the~~ Directed to **James Sinclare, Joseph S. Burch, William McBryde, Henry J. King** & **William Hancock** Requiring them or any three or more of them to Divide the Estate Real & personal of **Hardy Sellars Senr.** Deceased according to the the legal Rights of the parties under the provision of the will of **Hardy Sellars Senr.** and that said Commissioner do Report their proceedings thereon to this Court at its next sitting.   **Wm. Harper**

Levina Sellars   )
Hardy H. Sellars &   )
Zylpha Sellars   ) Bill for Accounts &
vs.   ) &
John Evans   )   )
Turner Bryan) Executors) Partition
& **John Sellars** & others   ) On motion of **Robbins** & **McIver** it is ordered that the Executors Accounts be Refered to the Commissioner of this court ~~anad~~ \and/ that he do Report thereon.   **Wm. Harper**

Exparte)   )
Thomas Summerford)
minor by next friend   ) On motion of **Wilkins** It is ordered that the Commissioner inquire and Report on the facts stated in this Petition.
Wm. Harper

Exparte   )
John F. Ervin) The Commissioner having Submitted his Report on the
Accounts of **Robt. Ervin** late Trustee of **Jesse Wilds** a Lunatic in which he
finds a balance of Eight hundred and forty Nine Dollars 54/100 Due by the
Est. of **Jesse Wilds** to the Est. of **Robt. Ervin** It is on motion of **Wilkins**
ordered that the said Report be confirmed.   **Wm. Harper**

Exparte   )
Eli H. Lide) The Commr. having \made/ a Report in this case on motion of
Sims ordered that the report be Confirmed.

Page 482   *January 1837*
January Term 1837

Exparte   )
Elisha Baker)
Guardian of   )
Sarah Baker) Ordered that the Rule against **Elisha Baker** for not making
his last annual Return be Discharged It appearing that the ward of the said
Elisha Baker ~~in~~ is now of age it \is/ ordered that ~~the~~ he be excused from
making any farther Returns to this Court as guardian.
W. Harper

Sarah Stubbs & others)
        vs.   ) Bill for Accounts & Partition
Daniel Stubbs & others) On motion of **Graham** it is ordered that the administrators be allowed to file the Accounts in this case forthwith.

Sarah Stubbs & others)
        vs.   ) Bill for Accounts & Partition
Daniel Stubbs & others) On motion of **Robbins** & **McIver** it is orderd that
the Administrators Account be Refered to the Commissioner of this Court
and that he do Report thereon.   **Wm. Harper**

Exparte   )
C. D. Wallace   )
Guardian   )
of **E. A. Ellerbe**   )
Margt. A. Ellerbe)
Thos. S. Wallace)
& **W. D. Wallace**   ) The Commissioner having Reported on this case it is on
motion of **Graham** Solicitor Confirmed.   **Wm. Harper**

Sarah Stubbs & others)
      vs.   ) Bill for Account & Partition
Daniel Stubbs & others) The Commissioner appointed by the order of this
court ~~to make partition~~ in this case to make partition of the Estate of **James Stubbs** having made their report in confirmity to the writ ~~of~~

Page 483   _January 1837_
                              January Term 1837

to them Directed it is on motion of **Robbins** & **McIver** ordered that <u>that</u> the same be confirmed.   **Wm. Harper**

The Court Then Adjourned till 11 oclock To morrow morning.

The Court met Pursuant to Adjournment.

Expartite   )
The Commr.)
in Equity   ) The Commissioner having Submitted his Report on Estates
Bonds &c in his hands it is ordered that the same be confirmed.

Expartite   ) Report guardians
The Commr.) The Commissioner having Submitted his Report on guardians who have ~~at~~ duly made their Returns it is ordered that the same be
confirmed.   **Wm. Harper**

Expartite   ) Report on Defaulting Guardians
The Commr.)
in Equity   ) The Commissioner having Submitted his Report upon
guardians who are in default with their Returns ~~and on~~ and upon such as are
otherwise in Default It is ordered that the said Report be confirmed and that
rule be issued against such guardians as are in default as aforesaid returnable
to the next court and that \attachment/ issue against guardians upon \whom
rules have been served/ ~~who have ser secured~~ and who have failed to ~~the~~
\return their/ account or make Returns to the Rules.
                                      W. Harper

Wm. H. Fraser & wife)
      vs.   ) Bill for Sales Partition Account &c.
Jim[?] **Gee** Admr.   )
P. R. Gee & others   ) On motion of **Wilkins** It is ordered that it be
Refered to the Commissioner of this court to <u>e</u>quire wheth the Sales of Real
Estate mentioned in said Bill is ~~a~~ beneficial to the Infant Defendant.
                                      Wm. Harper

January Term 1837

Exparte   )
Thomas Summerford) Petition for Exchange of Land
by his next friend   ) On motion of **Wilkins** It is ordered that the Report
be confirmed.   **W. Harper**

Administrator of **E. White**)
    vs.   ) Bill for Relief & Injunction
Creditors of **E. White**   ) On motion of **Sims** Complainants Solicitor it is
ordered that a writ of [*blot*]junction do ~~Issue~~ Issue directed to **C. R. Woods**
& **T. J. K. Dargan** Known as **C. R. Woods** and Company to **H. Stoddard** and
Phil N. Birch otherwise know as **Stoddard, Birch & Company** and **Moses
Butler** restraining them from all <u>all</u> further proceedings at common Law
against the Admr. of **Elisha White** Deceased and \that/ all others the credi-
tors of the said **White** be injoined from suing & \enforcing/ ~~reforming~~ &
Collection of their claims at Law It is also ordered that the creditors ~~Elish~~ of
Elisha White Deceased ~~don~~ do ~~make~~ Render in to the the Commissioner of
this court and prove their claims before him before the first day of June next
and further that this order be published for three months in the Cheraw
Gazette.   **W. Harper**

Exparte   ) Petition for Guardianship
Elias Windham) The Commissioner to whom this Petition was Refered to
Report on the facts therein stated and also as to the fitness of the petitioner to
act as Guardian of the Estate of his Children and as to the amount for which
~~put~~ \he should give/ Bond ~~give Bond~~ having made his Report on motion of
Sims Solicitor for petitioner It is ordered that the Report of the Commis-
sioner be confirmed and that the Petitioner **Elias Windham** be appointed
Guardian of the Estate of his sons **Postell C. Windham** and **Richard E.
Windham** upon his giving Bond to ~~to~~ the Commissioner of this Court with
Security to be approved of by said Commissioner in the penal sum of Six
Thousand Dollars Conditioned for the faithful performance of his Duty as
Guardian as Aforesaid.   **Wm. Harper**

[*end of book*]

Index

Name appears on page as "Same," carried over from previous page

†Name appears on page more than once   *‡Name appears on all pages more than once*

Name appears on page as "Same," carried over from previous page

[†]*Name appears on page more than once*   [‡]*Name appears on all pages more than once*

*Name appears on page as "Same," carried over from previous page

†*Name appears on page more than once*   ‡*Name appears on all pages more than once*

*Name appears on page as "Same," carried over from previous page

†*Name appears on page more than once*   ‡*Name appears on all pages more than once*

Genealogical books by the author
Lee G. Barrow
4071 Ada Creek Dr.
Gainesville, GA 30506
bargraphica.com/books

Cheraw District, South Carolina, Court of Equity, Minutes Volume 1: 1801-1823. Volume 2: Minutes, 1823-1832. Volume 3: 1833-1837
Includes executors, administrators, heirs, guardians, estate petitions and other equity records for Cheraw District, which included present-day Chesterfield, Darlington, Marlboro and portions of Florence and Lee Counties. A valuable source of information about relationships, ages, date of decease and other facts about persons who lived in the area. Full-name index with over 1,200 names in each volume.

Court Records of Williamsburg County, South Carolina, Volume 1: Court of Common Pleas, Rough Journals, 1814-1821. Includes lists of jurors, county officers, guardians, executors, estate petitions and other court cases from 1814 to 1821. A valuable source of information about relationships, locations, ages, and other facts about persons in Williamsburg County (which at the time included portions of present day Florence County). Full-name index with over 1,500 names.

Early Court Records of Pulaski County, Georgia, 1809-1825.
The earliest records of Pulaski County (including present-day Bleckley and Dodge Counties). Juror Lists, Superior Court Minutes, Inferior Court Minutes, Court of Ordinary Minutes, Letters of Administration, Administrators, Executors, and Guardians. Full name index with over 2,500 names.

Richmond County, North Carolina, Court Minutes: Court of Pleas and Quarter Sessions, Minute Book 1, 1779-1786. The earliest minute book of the Court of Pleas and Quarter Sessions of Richmond County (including present-day Scotland County). Deed registrations, suits, jury lists, county officers, will recordings, guardianships, estate settlements, road crews, etc. Full name index with 1,000 names.

Richmond County, North Carolina, Court Minutes: Court of Pleas and Quarter Sessions, Minute Book 2, 1786-1792. The second minute book of the Court of Pleas and Quarter Sessions of Richmond County (including present-day Scotland County). Deed registrations, suits, jury lists, county officers, will recordings, guardianships, estate settlements, road crews, etc. Full name index with 1,000 names.

Stewart County, Georgia, Superior Court Minutes, Volume 1, 1829-1834.
The first minute book of the Superior Court of Stewart County, including some early records for present-day Quitman, Randolph, Webster and portions of Clay, Marion and Terrell Counties. Juror lists, suits, divorces, debts, land disputes, criminal prosecutions and other court cases for the years 1829 to 1834. Full name index with over 900 names.

Stewart County, Georgia, Superior Court Minutes, Volume 2, 1835-1839.
The second minute book of the Superior Court of Stewart County, including records for present-day Webster and portions of Marion and Quitman Counties. Juror lists, suits, divorces, debts, land disputes, criminal prosecutions and other court cases for the years 1835 to 1839. Full name index with nearly 2,000 names.

Williamsburg County, South Carolina, Voter Registration Book, 1882-1892. Voter registrations for the entirety of Williamsburg County, showing name, age, occupation, and place of residence. A valuable replacement for the lost 1890 census and important source of information on those who lived in this area at the end of the 19th century. Full name index with almost 6,000 names.